March 16, 1993

May the Lord bless you
and keep you —
while we are absent
one from the other.
Your 8:30 A. M. Prayer Partners,

Lonnie Wascom

Ruth P. Keen
Dorothy Gunn
Opal Roe Wild

Layman's Bible Book Commentary
Proverbs, Ecclesiastes, Song of Solomon

LAYMAN'S BIBLE BOOK COMMENTARY

PROVERBS, ECCLESIASTES,
SONG OF SOLOMON
VOLUME 9

L. D. Johnson

BROADMAN PRESS
Nashville, Tennessee

4211-79

ISBN: 0-8054-1179-8

Dewey Decimal Classification: 223.7

Subject headings: BIBLE. O. T. PROVERBS//BIBLE. O. T. ECCLESIASTES//
BIBLE. O. T. SONG OF SOLOMON

Library of Congress Catalog Card Number: 80-66543

Printed in the United States of America

Foreword

The *Layman's Bible Book Commentary* in twenty-four volumes was planned as a practical exposition of the whole Bible for lay readers and students. It is based on the conviction that the Bible speaks to every generation of believers but needs occasional reinterpretation in the light of changing language and modern experience. Following the guidance of God's Spirit, the believer finds in it the authoritative word for faith and life.

To meet the needs of lay readers, the *Commentary* is written in a popular style, and each Bible book is clearly outlined to reveal its major emphases. Although the writers are competent scholars and reverent interpreters, they have avoided critical problems and the use of original languages except where they were essential for explaining the text. They recognize the variety of literary forms in the Bible, but they have not followed documentary trails or become preoccupied with literary concerns. Their primary purpose was to show what each Bible book meant for its time and what it says to our own generation.

The Revised Standard Version of the Bible is the basic text of the *Commentary*, but writers were free to use other translations to clarify an occasional passage or sharpen its effect. To provide as much interpretation as possible in such concise books, the Bible text was not printed along with the comment.

Of the twenty-four volumes of the *Commentary*, fourteen deal with Old Testament books and ten with those in the New Testament. The volumes range in pages from 140 to 168. Four major books in the Old Testament and five in the New are treated in one volume each. Others appear in various combinations. Although the allotted space varies, each Bible book is treated as a whole to reveal its basic message with some passages getting special attention. Whatever plan of Bible study the reader may follow, this *Commentary* will be a valuable companion.

Despite the best-seller reputation of the Bible, the average survey of Bible knowledge reveals a good deal of ignorance about it and its primary meaning. Many adult church members seem to think that its study is intended for children and preachers. But some of the newer translations have been making the Bible more readable for all ages. Bible study has branched out from Sunday into other days of the week, and into neighborhoods rather than just in churches. This *Commentary* wants to meet the growing need for insight into all that the Bible has to say about God and his world and about Christ and his fellowship.

BROADMAN PRESS

Contents

ECCLESIASTES

SONG OF SOLOMON

Introduction

Three streams fed the river of Israel's religious understanding: the priest, the prophet, and the wise. Priests represented the life of worship. Israel looked to her priests for the practice of the mystery of faith in the acts of devotion. Nearly all of Leviticus and the last fifteen chapters of Exodus describe in detail the function of the priest as worship leader. Many biblical interpreters have not appreciated the wealth and significance of liturgy and ritual in Old Testament worship. Tabernacle and ark, altar and incense, were the priest's province. Whatever had to do with the offering of sacrifice, by which the Hebrew understood himself to make atonement for sins, was presided over by the priest. The mystery of God made known in a sacred place, a curtained holy of holies, an altar of sacrifice, the odor of animal blood and burning incense, all related to the priestly function. He was a separated person who, when he wore his vestments, mediated the divine gift of forgiveness and restoration.

The power of the priesthood was connected with the Temple in Jerusalem. Twenty-four "courses" or groups of priests took turns providing the daily services of sacrifice. As long as the Temple remained as the visible symbol of God's presence, the priest occupied a strategic place in Israel's religious life. The Babylonians sacked Jerusalem in 586 BC, destroying the Temple, and from that date until 520-516, when a modest Temple was constructed, there was no holy place. Moreover, for much of that period Israel's leaders lived in exile in Babylon. In the interim, Scripture replaced the nonexistent Temple as the focus of Israel's religious expression, and the priest either became or was succeeded by the teacher. Thus when Ezra came from Babylon to Jerusalem about 428 BC, it is difficult to tell whether he was primarily a priest or a teacher. He brought a copy of the Book of the Law and instructed the people as to God's requirements of them. But he also supervised the service of sacrifice

11

in the Temple, which had been rebuilt almost a hundred years earlier at the urging of the prophets Haggai and Zechariah.

That plain and unimpressive structure, often referred to as the "Second Temple," was replaced after five hundred years by the magnificent building constructed by Herod the Great. Herod's Temple was, of course, the one known and visited by Jesus.

The abuses of Temple worship denounced by the prophets and our Lord influence our attitudes toward priestly religion. It is tempting for persons in a nonliturgical, nonpriestly tradition to find little merit in priesthood. However, much connected with the Temple was devoutly religious. The facts that Jesus himself was dedicated as an infant by his mother in the Temple and that he regarded it as a sacred place are not to be forgotten. His extreme action in driving the money changers from the Temple area was not prompted by petulance but by his profound respect for the house of God. "Is it not written," he charged, 'My house shall be called a house of prayer for all the nations'? But you have made it a den of robbers" (Mark 11:17). As long as the Temple stood, it remained a significant aspect of Israel's faith, and the priests held an influential place in Hebrew religious thought.

The second stream composing the river of Hebrew religion was prophetic. Early prophetism in Israel was often highly ecstatic, its practitioners akin to whirling dervishes roving in bands about the countryside, going into trances to make predictions for those who paid them money. An example of this type of early prophetism is reported in 1 Samuel 10:5-13, and again in 1 Samuel 19:18-24. In both instances Saul participated in a form of ecstatic behavior, along with a "band of prophets" (10:5) described as prophesying to the accompaniment of musical instruments—"harp, tambourine, flute, and lyre." The frenzied ecstatics used the rhythmic sounds produced by the instruments to induce the trance from which they engaged in fortune-telling.

The relationship between that kind of behavior and the messages of an Amos or an Isaiah is about as close as that between a snake-handling group in a camp meeting and the services of St. Paul's Cathedral. By the time of King David, Saul's successor, prophetism began to emerge from the whirling-dervish trance performance into responsible speaking for Yahweh. Such figures as Nathan, Gad, Micaiah, Elijah, and Elisha played responsible roles in the nation's moral and political life. None of those men left documents conserving their messages. What we know of their prophetic work has come down to us through the inspired history in the Old Testament.

Beginning about 750 BC, a number of the prophets of the Lord left written messages, as well as delivering oral ones. In the eighth century BC, four towering prophetic figures are found. In Israel there were Amos and Hosea; in Judah, Isaiah and Micah. Men such as Zephaniah and Nahum belonged to the seventh century BC, while Jeremiah and Ezekiel began their work in the seventh and continued on into the sixth century, the time of the Exile of Judah to Babylon. Such prophets as Haggai and Zachariah came to Judah after the restoration from captivity. Malachi and one or two others belong to the fifth century BC. Then prophecy ceased. As the prophet had arisen by God's providence, his work was replaced by the teacher.

Although they were allies and colaborers in the religious life of God's people, priests and prophets were not always on the most cordial terms. Indeed, the prophets were frequently highly critical of the priests, and of the teachers, too. No doubt the prophets were often considered by the priests to be enemies of established religion. The confrontation between Amaziah, the priest of Bethel, and the prophet Amos, reported in Amos 7:10-17, is a case in point. Another is Jeremiah's clash with the priests of his own family in Anathoth (Jer. 11:21-23). Consider these words of Hosea, Amos's contemporary: "As robbers lie in wait for a man,/so the priests are banded together;/they murder on the way to Shechem,/yea, they commit villainy" (6:9). Harsh accusation. Isaiah, also of the eighth century, was appalled by the drunkenness of priests and prophets in Jerusalem. In their alcoholic stupor they had the effrontery to tell the people how to live (28:7-8). Micah, Isaiah's contemporary, accused the priests and prophets of teaching and divining "for hire" (3:11). In the seventh century Zephaniah denounced both priests and prophets for "profan[ing] what is sacred" (3:4). Jeremiah, his ministry lasting about a half century (627-580), continually accused Jerusalem's priests of being part of the deadly conspiracy that was leading the nation to destruction. See Jeremiah 1:18; 2:8; 2:26; 4:9; 5:31; 8:1; 13:13. Also read Lamentations 4:13,16 for examples of Jeremiah's view of the calamity of professional priesthood. Jeremiah's younger contemporary, Ezekiel, was himself a priest as well as a prophet, but on at least one occasion he denounced the priesthood (Ezek. 22:26). Malachi, post-Exilic prophet of the fifth century BC, was deeply devoted to the Temple and respected the vocation of priesthood, but the cynical professionalism of priests in his day outraged him. He said that the Lord says, "O priests, who despise my name" (1:6). The scriptural evidence that the prophets did not hold the profession of priesthood in high esteem is impressive.

Nor were some of the prophets uncritical of the "wise," the third and least known of the three streams feeding Israel's religious understanding. Isaiah questioned the wise for their admiration of Egypt's governmental skills and power (30:1-2; 31:1-2; 19:11-12). In his famous list of "woes" Isaiah included those "who are wise in their own eyes" (5:21). Jeremiah was even sharper in his criticism of the wise, inasmuch as he saw them as advisers to the court having a leading part in the conspiracy that would destroy Judah. See Jeremiah 9:23-24 and 18:18 for examples of such opposition to the leaders of the nation, including the wise.

But who were "the wise?" Were they a distinct and recognized group, or is the word only the designation of any person who showed himself or herself to have acquired unusual understanding of life? The answer is both. Wisdom, in Hebrew *hokmah*, has numerous usages in the Old Testament. Often it means technical skill and dexterity. Exodus commonly uses the term to describe the skilled work of craftsmen making the tabernacle and utensils for worship (28:3; 35:25,31,35; 36:4). Men like Bezalel, a craftsman, are called "wise." Solomon asked Hiram of Tyre to send a man "skilled [wise] to work in gold, silver," and other precious metals in the building of the Temple (2 Chron. 2:7). Solomon's special competence (wisdom) as a ruler and administrator is celebrated in 1 Kings 5:7,12.

Further, the same word, *hokmah*, is sometimes taken to mean shrewdness, not skill; craftiness, not craftsmanship; cunning rather than competence. Thus, Amnon ravished his half-sister, Tamar, by using a scheme devised by his friend, Jonadab, described as a very "crafty" [wise] man (2 Sam. 13:3). Joab employed a "wise" (clever) woman of Tekoa to convince King David to restore his exiled son, Absalom (2 Sam. 14:2). In 1 Kings 2:6, the dying David admonishes his chosen successor, Solomon, to use his "wisdom" (cunning) to dispose of the dangerous Joab, who had sided with Adonijah against Solomon in the succession struggle.

Another meaning of *hokmah* in the Old Testament is intellectual power and encyclopedic knowledge. Thus Solomon's wisdom is described in 1 Kings 4:20-34 by citing his astonishing composition of 3,000 proverbs and 1,005 songs. In 1 Kings 10:6-7, the queen of Sheba tells Solomon that she has heard in her land "of your affairs and of your wisdom," but confesses in wonderment that "the half was not told me."

A fourth and more frequent use of the word in the Old Testament refers to moral discernment. Thus Solomon, in an inaugural prayer, asked the Lord "that I may discern [be wise] between good and evil," and

God answered by saying, "I give you a wise and discerning mind" (1 Kings 3:9,12). Another example of wisdom as moral discernment is in Deuteronomy 1:13, where Moses recalled that he had appointed leaders who were "wise, understanding, and experienced." They had more than the capacity to make clever decisions; they also knew how to make right ones.

The ultimate quality of wisdom is reverence for the Lord, and such a definition of wisdom is found in numerous places in the Old Testament, including Proverbs 1:7; 2:6; 9:10; 15:33; Job 28:28; and Psalm 111:10. Here the focus is not on people and how to manipulate the environment successfully by knowing how things work or by sheer cleverness. Rather, the focus is on God as the source of wisdom, and a person's need to worship and obey him.

It is significant that there is a refinement and progression in the meanings of wisdom in the Old Testament—from skill and dexterity, to cleverness and cunning, to intellectual acumen, to moral discernment, and, finally, to reverence for the Lord and obedience to his Word. In some late writings in Proverbs and in some of the apocryphal Wisdom writings there is yet another meaning given to *wisdom*. It is pictured as a personified God-like quality, not unlike an eternal spiritual entity in itself. In the study of Proverbs 8:22-31, we shall encounter this conception.

We have reviewed the several usages of the word *hokmah*, wisdom, in the Old Testament, and we now turn our attention to the Old Testament literature which is known as Wisdom. This is found principally in the Books of Proverbs, Job, Ecclesiastes, and certain of the Psalms, such as 1, 37, 49, 73, 111, 112, 119. In the Aprocrypha, written in the intertestamental period, there are also two books of wisdom writing, the Wisdom of Jesus the Son of Sirach (Ecclesiasticus), and the Wisdom of Solomon. What makes a writing "wisdom" rather than prophecy or history? Wisdom as a literary form is distinguished by its presuppositions. It presupposes that conclusions about life may be reached from the observation of experience and the rational reflection upon such observations. While the prophet is announcing, "Thus saith the Lord," the wise man is saying, "The widespread experience of people, confirmed by my own observation and reflection, is that such-and-such is true." Thus the distinguishing characteristic of wisdom writing is assurance that mankind is endowed by God with rationality to observe life and draw valid conclusions which serve as guidelines for successful and happy living. It would not be an exaggeration to describe the difference between the prophet's and the wise person's approach to truth as the two beams of a cross. The prophet's message is vertical, coming down from God. "Thus saith the Lord" is his theme. The wise arrives at truth from the horizontal plane. It is not that he does not believe in Yahweh or worship him, but he believes that the eternal truths of God are written in the human experience. What are the conclusions of common human experience? Those are the focus of wisdom writing. That is the reason that wisdom writing lends itself to short, pithy admonitions or observations, such as are found in the Book of Proverbs. These are conclusions, or they are instructions. For the most part, the proverb writer does not argue. He declares; he admonishes; he instructs; he gives the reader a distilled summation of a great deal of experience about life.

However, there are two varieties of Old Testament wisdom writing, both based upon the principle of rational reflection upon experience. The first is practical, primarily represented in Proverbs. This practical, down-to-earth wisdom is confident that God has organized life to work in certain ways, that these ways are knowable to people, and that failure to live in these established ways leads to disaster. A second type of Old Testament wisdom is found in Job and Ecclesiastes. It is less positive about knowable conclusions concerning the way life works. As in Proverbs, the writers of this literature of questioning base their claims upon experience and rationality. However, they are much less certain about the orderliness and predictability of human affairs. For example, one of the Wisdom psalms declares, "I have been young, and now am old;/yet I have not seen the righteous forsaken/or his children begging bread" (Ps. 37:25). But in a passionate outcry Job laments the condition of the righteous poor and concludes with the awful accusation, "Yet God pays no attention to their prayer" (Job 24:1-12)! And the chief message of Qoheleth, writer of the Book of Ecclesiastes, is that if there is a divine moral order it is unknowable to man, and that man cannot by experience or rationality come to any reliable conclusions about a transcendent meaning to life. Such are some of the dimensions of Old Testament wisdom writing.

In this volume we shall study one of each of the two types of wisdom—the practical and the questioning, Proverbs representing the former, Ecclesiastes the latter. In addition, we shall examine the writing known as Song of Solomon, which is not a wisdom writing but is sometimes included with these writings because Solomon's name is identified with the title. As we shall see, this is really a series of love songs.

PROVERBS

Introduction

The Book of Proverbs was designed as a vehicle for teaching Israel's youth the collected wisdom of their forebears. As today's youth are using computers for memory banks, the ancient employed the device of proverbs to preserve bits and pieces of the conclusions which generations had reached out of their experience. The special quality of the proverb is that it is an artful, rhythmic, brief, often delightfully "catchy" way of summing up something about the nature of God, the world, and human nature.

Turn to the Book of Proverbs and begin reading at chapter 10. Notice that the material is almost entirely composed of brief, two-line, pithy observations or admonitions. Each separate two-line saying is a gem to be held up before the mind's eye, examined, and cherished. Seldom is there a logical connection between one proverb and its predecessor or successor. The proverbs are like pearls strung together to form an exquisite and luminous necklace. Except for chapters 1—9, 30—31, the entire book is a collection of mostly two-line (some four-line) sayings. The proverb is not an intricate, detailed, step-by-step logical statement of evidence supporting a certain conclusion. The proverb *is* the conclusion, given in such a literary form as to be easily remembered. It is a highly concentrated capsule of an enormous amount of human experience.

Such "folk wisdom," the pithy expression of a people's experience, is found in nearly every developed culture. We have our own store of it in America. "A stitch in time saves nine." "Waste not, want not." Note the characteristics of such sayings. For one thing, we inherited them. They represent not just the views of one person, but are common property. Their origin may be uncertain, but their validity is unchallenged. Secondly, the sayings are artfully refined to give the essence of a truth. Examine "Waste not, want not." The proverb has the virtues of brevity, apt positioning of cause (waste) and consequence (want), and vividness.

The important thing to remember about the proverb is that it produces no surprises in the reader. One is not apt to say about a proverb, "I didn't know that!" On the other hand, the proverb produces the feeling, "Why, of course that is true! What a fine way to say it!"

It should come as no surprise, therefore, that the writing of wisdom in proverb form is one of the most common features of the literature of ancient Israel's neighbors. In fact, much of such wisdom writing antedates Israel's wisdom by centuries. This is not to suggest that the Old Testament writings are not God-inspired. It is to point out that the form and style of such writing is not unique to the Old Testament.

Obviously, not all proverbs are religious in nature, except in the broadest sense of the word that all truth, wherever found, is believed by the religious person to have its origin in God and in his law of the universe. The Old Testament proverbs, in fact, are not primarily directed toward explaining the nature of God, but toward explaining how life works. *Consequences* is a key word to an understanding of the Book of Proverbs. The Book says "Don't do this," "Do do that," because predictable consequences follow either action.

The predictability of God's world is basic to the Book of Proverbs. This is God's world; he made and controls it; he is orderly and does not act capriciously. Therefore, if you do right you may expect good results. If you do wrong you may expect to suffer bad consequences. It is this certainty about the moral law which makes Proverbs such a positive religious force. This is no speculative writing about the ambiguities and uncertainties of human existence. Leave that to Qoheleth and Job. In this book the answers are categorical and plain. As you read Proverbs, notice the simplicity and certainty of its conclusions.

That there are moral consequences to one's behavior is at the heart of the Old Testament. God's people were in covenant relation with him. He offered the terms of the covenant; Israel could accept or reject, obey or disobey. Obedience brought blessing, disobedience punishment. Read 2 Chronicles 7:14 for a classic statement of the reward-retribution motif of the Old Testament's understanding of covenant relationship with the Lord.

The prophets upheld the covenant conception of Israel's relationship with Yahweh. The image of God as husband and Israel as wife, or of the Lord as father and Israel as child, is common in the prophets' preaching and writing. Consider Hosea as illustrative. Hosea's personal tragedy with an unfaithful wife is seen by the prophet as a microcosm of the cosmic tragedy of God with an unfaithful chosen one, Israel. Behind the theology of the prophets is the conviction of God's covenant with Israel, a covenant expressed in definable, predictable rewards for obedience and punishments for disobedience.

The same covenant message of a dependable system in which righteousness is rewarded and wickedness is punished will be found in Proverbs. There are two important differences, however, between the focus of the Book of Proverbs and the covenant writings of the prophets or Deuteronomy. One is that the Proverbs are based upon a universal law, that is, they assume that the observations and admonitions which are directed to the Israelite youth would be applicable as well for any other young man. Life works the same for an Israelite or a non-Israelite, because God is the God of all. The other difference one notes is that the Proverbs are primarily concerned with individual morality, while the prophets and the other Old Testament covenant writings are mainly directed toward Israel as a people. The individual is the focus of Proverbs; the nation is the focus of Deuteronomy, Kings, Chronicles and the prophets. Proverbs, then, is a book of instructions telling one how to live as an individual in order to reap the benefits of an order established by God and universally binding man to its obedience.

Look again at the text of the Book of Proverbs. Note that its form is poetic, rather than prosaic. Hebrew poetry does not sound like poetry to an American reader because it does not use rhyme as a means of carrying the force of the thought. Hebrew poetry uses rhythm and parallelism. By rhythm we mean that there is a certain cadence to the writing, each line having three or two beats. Much of the sense of cadence is lost in translation, of course, but it is a primary characteristic of Hebrew poetry, holding the lines together in much the same way as is done in English poetry through the use of rhyme. Occasionally the thought is accented by the use of alliteration.

The other characteristic of Hebrew poetry is a simple device of putting two lines together in a certain position to one another. The parallelism makes a complete thought, the first line introducing an idea to which the second line relates. Three specific forms of parallelism are found in Proverbs: synonymous, antithetic, and synthetic. The synonymous parallelism puts the two lines of a saying together in such a way that the second line is an echo of the first, reinforcing the thought expressed by the first. Two examples of this type of thought expression may be noted in Proverbs 16:18,32. The first is the familiar observation, "Pride goes before destruction,/and a haughty spirit before a fall." The other reads, "He who is slow to anger is better than the mighty,/and he who rules his spirit than he who takes a city." Notice that in each case the second line simply restates to reinforce the thought of the first.

The second type of parallelism is the most common in Proverbs. It is appropriately called antithetic, for the second line states the contrasting side of the claim made by the first line, the two lines often connected by the conjunction "but." Some 90 percent of the proverbs in Proverbs 10—15 are of this form. Consider these two well-known proverbs: "Righteousness exalts a nation,/but sin is a reproach to any people" (14:34); "A soft answer turns away wrath,/but a harsh word stirs up anger" (15:1). The second line in each case has stated the opposite side of the first.

A third type of parallelism is sometimes called "synthetic," or "progressive." In this type of proverb the second line advances or completes the thought of the first. Consider this homespun observation: "The beginning of strife is like letting out water;/so quit before the quarrel breaks out" (17:14). Or read this couplet: "Wine is a mocker, strong drink a brawler;/and whoever is led astray by it is not wise" (20:1). The second line has accentuated and elaborated the meaning of the first.

Besides the three literary arrangements of two-line parallelisms, there are other forms in which thought is expressed in proverbs. One is a two-line verse of comparison, usually expressed in the form, "Better this than that." "Better is a man of humble standing who works for himself/than one who plays the great man but lacks bread" (12:9). "Better is a little with righteousness/than great revenues with injustice" (16:8). "It is better to live in a desert land/than with a contentious and fretful woman" (21:19).

Yet another proverb form is the similitude, in which two things are said to be "like" each other, the comparison accentuating the nature of the thing described. "A word fitly spoken/is like apples of gold in a setting of silver" (25:11) accentuates the value of apt speech. "Like the glaze covering an earthen vessel/are smooth lips with an evil heart" (26:23) is a dramatic description of the deceit of smooth-talking wickedness.

Another form of the proverb is numerical. The writer chooses a subject, say, "Things the Lord hates." Then he makes a list of things the Lord hates. Next, for poetic effect he subtracts one, then adds it at the end of his list. Consider the following: "There are six things which the Lord hates,/seven which are an abomination to him:/haughty eyes,/a lying tongue,/and hands that shed innocent blood,/a heart that devises wicked plans,/feet that make haste to run to evil,/a false witness who breathes out lies,/and a man who sows discord among brothers"

(6:16-19). A series of numerical proverbs is found in chapter 30.

Often a proverb is a simple observation about some slice of experience, distilling the conclusion reached at the end of long and painful living. Consider this bit of bitter parental experience: "A stupid son is a grief to a father;/and the father of a fool has no joy" (17:21). Even more often than observation, a proverb may be in the form of admonition. "My son, be attentive to my words" (4:20) is a frequent introduction to a warning. Consider this admonition: "Make no friendship with a man given to anger,/nor go with a wrathful man,/lest you learn his ways" (22:24). A third form of proverb is the paradox, an observation that something is really true although it appears to be contradictory. "He who loves him [his son] is diligent to discipline him" (13:24). But ask the son if discipline feels like love.

It has been noted that Proverbs is chiefly a collection of two-and-four-line sayings, but one considerable exception is to be made to that generality. Chapters 1—9, by many scholars said to be the last part of the book to be written, are a collection of long teaching poems, some twelve in all. This section begins with the title, a statement of the purposes of the book (1:2-6), and a theme for the entire book (1:7). Then follow discourses upon several subjects related to the proper upbringing of a young man. Among these are a statement of the value of such proper teaching as a moral safeguard (1:8-19); the personification of wisdom as a prophetess who denounces folly and wickedness (1:20-33); the benefits of wisdom (ch. 2); the praise of wisdom (ch. 4); warnings against becoming involved with a "loose woman," and the virtues of monogamy (ch. 5); warnings against certain ordinary human frailties such as laziness (6:1-19); further warnings against the adulteress (6:20 to 7:27); presentation of wisdom as a prophetess who was with the Lord at the beginning of creation (ch. 8); and a final contrast of wisdom and folly (ch. 9).

At the conclusion of the Book of Proverbs there are several additional poems which contrast with the two-and-four-line style of the body of the book. Chapter 30:1-9 is a dialogue with a skeptic. Chapter 30:10-33 contains a number of short admonitions put together with a series of numerical proverbs. Chapter 31:1-9 is a warning addressed to a young prince by his mother. Then there is that lovely acrostic poem describing the ideal wife in the last chapter (31:10-31). Throughout these poems a note of moral earnestness will be found. The wisdom urged upon the reader is ethical obedience rather than intellectual achievement. The knowledge which is of value is knowledge of the way to live as the Lord has ordained the world, not mere cleverness about how to make the system work. Wisdom is God's gift to those dedicated to morality.

If you look once again at the Book of Proverbs as a whole, you discover that it is a collection of teaching materials held together by a common theme, namely that "The fear of the Lord is the beginning of wisdom,/and the knowledge of the Holy One is insight" (9:10). A wide variety of sources and periods in time may be seen by simply thumbing through the chapters to notice the several different titles and ascriptions within the overall covering introduction of 1:1-6. Chapter 10 begins with the simple ascription, "The proverbs of Solomon." This is the second "book" within the Book of Proverbs, and it ends at chapter 22:16. The third collection begins at 22:17 with the words, "Incline your ear, and hear the words of the wise,/and apply your mind to my knowledge." Here the two-line format changes to a four-line proverb. Another collection begins at 24:23, with the words, "These also are sayings of the wise." Chapters 25—29 are entitled "These also are proverbs of Solomon which the men of Hezekiah king of Judah copied" (25:1). We therefore know that the date of their collection, assuming that their origin is Solomonic, is not Solomon's time of the tenth century BC, but of the late eighth century BC, the time of King Hezekiah, a contemporary of the prophet Isaiah. Chapter 30 is introduced with the words, "The words of Agur son of Jakeh of Massa" (30:1*a*). "Massa" is the name of a tribe in Arabia, suggesting that the origin of this short collection is outside of Israel. An alternate translation of "Massa" is "oracle," which would make the place of origin of this collection unknown. A similar situation is found at the introduction of the final collection in Proverbs, chapter 31, introduced with the ascription, "The words of Lemuel, king of Massa, which his mother taught him" (v. 1).

What, then, is King Solomon's role in the formation of the Book of Proverbs? First Kings 4:30-34 tells us that Solomon was the father and patron of wisdom in Israel. He is acclaimed as having wisdom which "surpassed the wisdom of all the people of the east, and all the wisdom of Egypt" (1 Kings 4:30). That verse tells us that wisdom was a recognized gift of expression among peoples of "the east" and of Egypt, a culture much older than Israelite. But Solomon became famous for his wisdom. In 1 Kings 10:1-13 a visit from "the queen of Sheba," probably located in southwest Arabia (modern Yemen), is reported. She came "to test him with hard questions" (v. 1), telling him that she had heard in her own land "of your affairs and of your wisdom" (v. 6), but she went away in astonishment at his "wisdom and prosperity" (v. 7). First Kings 10:23

reports that "King Solomon excelled all the kings of the earth in riches and in wisdom." There is no question but that Solomon is to be identified with the development of wisdom in Israel.

It should also be noted that two of the times when the influence of Egypt was highest in Jerusalem wisdom flourished in Israel. The first was during the reign of Solomon, who took many wives, but whose principal wife was Egyptian. Further, he patterned his own court after the highly literate and bureaucratic organization in Egyptian government, importing ideas and personnel from Egypt to organize his own state affairs. That this was not highly popular with the people is attested to by the revolt which occurred after Solomon's death. The point is that wisdom, the knowledge of the world and how it operates under God's laws, the literate preservation and teaching of the lessons of life, was characteristic of Egypt before the time of Solomon. He himself became a patron of wisdom and its greatest exponent in Israel's history. It seems likely that the presence of Egyptian advisers and literary figures at Solomon's court spurred the wisdom movement in Israel.

Proverbs 25—29 is introduced by the statement that "These also are proverbs of Solomon which the men of Hezekiah king of Judah copied." Evidently there was a new interest in wisdom sayings in Judah during Hezekiah's time. It is also interesting that Hezekiah had close ties with Egypt in his struggle against the other big power of his day, Assyria. In fact, the prophet Isaiah was deeply distressed that Hezekiah was relying upon and closely allied with the Egyptians (Isa. 30:1-7; 31:1-3). It is interesting that on both occasions of Egyptian influence in Israel wisdom flourished. The entire Book of Proverbs may have been compiled after the Exile.

Book I

1:1 to 9:18

Title, Introduction, and Motto (1:1-7)

The title of Proverbs is intended to connect the entire collection with the name of King Solomon, although it is quite evident from within the book itself that Solomon is not the sole author. The introduction states the writer's purpose to provide a textbook for the moral guidance and intellectual growth of youth, and at the same time serve as a source of study and inspiration for the spiritually mature. In a series of clauses, all related to the title and forming a complete sentence, the purposes of the book are listed. "That men may know" (v. 2) assumes that knowing what is right is a prerequisite and motive for doing right. You cannot be expected to do right simply by instinct; someone has to teach you right from wrong. "Wisdom" (*hokmah*) has numerous meanings, as noted in the Introduction, but here it means knowledge of the moral law of God. "Instruction," which is coupled with wisdom, has a basic meaning of discipline, or chastisement, and here it refers to the discipline (perhaps sometimes accompanied by punishment for lessons unlearned) to which one must submit oneself in order to learn the laws of God. The root meaning of *understand* is to separate, or divide. (See 2 Tim. 2:15, KJV.) "Understanding," therefore, is the ability to separate the wheat from the chaff, good from evil.

"Receive" (v. 3) reminds us that much of what we know is a gift handed down from the past. To ignore the past is to condemn ourselves to repeat its errors. The teacher's function is to introduce us to the accumulated lessons of the past, so that we do not have to repeat the total human experience in each generation. Next follow in the text a list of areas in which instruction is to be received. "Wise dealing" in this context means good common sense about how to conduct the affairs of life. How does one show good common sense? By the practice of righteousness, justice, and equity. "Righteousness" may be understood as personal conduct which is right as God has given us the right. "Justice" is right conduct in respect to others and their rights. "Equity" is something of a combination of the two—personal morality and social justice—and means about what we mean when we say that a person is "on the level," or "straight as an arrow."

Verse 4 states the writer's second set of purposes in this book of wisdom. "Prudence" means what we mean by *savvy*, being wise to the ways and wiles of evil so that one is not misled. Such education is to be given to the "simple," that is, the inexperienced but teachable. The Book of Proverbs employs several words which are translated as *simple*, or simply *fool*. Each one has a separate meaning, some derogatory, others merely descriptive of youthful naiveté. Here the latter meaning is meant. The writer is talking about the youth who is unlearned and therefore open to being influenced, both by good and evil. Remember, not to teach good is to expose those who are inexperienced to the world of evil. "Discretion" ties in with prudence. It means the power of discrimination, and the ability to chart one's own course, knowing where the shoals lie.

Verse 5 introduces another reason for this writing. The key word here is "also." These writings are not for the eyes, mind, and heart of the inexperienced alone. They are also profitable for the wise, the learned, and intelligent. Such people can "increase in learning" and "acquire skill," a word which comes from seamanship, and means being skilled in the management of one's boat of life. Verse 6 enumerates ways in which the wise man by use of this wisdom will increase his learning and skill. It will help him understand "proverbs," "figures" (parables), sayings "of the wise," and "riddles" (sayings which have hidden meanings).

Verse 7 gives us the motto of the entire book. It comes after the brief introductory statement of the writer's purpose. Before setting forth the teachings, the writer summarizes his philosophy of wisdom. "Fear" means awe, or reverence. "Beginning" means either the starting point, or the most important part. Both meanings may be in the mind of the writer. True knowledge starts with and is dependent upon reverence of the Lord. By way of contrast, consider the "fools" (here the word is not simply the unlearned or uninitiated, but dull, swinish, thick-skulled, without sensitivity). A harsh but vivid description of this kind of fool is found in Porverbs 26:11: "Like a dog that returns to his vomit/is a fool that repeats his folly." There is no doubt that wisdom in the Old Testament endorses reverence for the Lord as essential to the living of the good life. (See Prov. 9:10; 15:33; Ps. 111:10; Job 28:28; Eccl. 12:13 for variations on this theme.)

Warning About Choosing Companions (1:8-19)

Verses 8-19 comprise the first long teaching poem of the first section of Proverbs, chapters 1—9. In this poem there are several warnings to the youth about the kind of companions he associates with. The poem begins with an exhortation to listen carefully to the teaching of the parents. Teaching of the young began with the parents and was continued by the wise (teachers). Don't reject their instruction, the youth is admonished. Do not think of the teaching as a burden and a reproach, but rather as a beautiful adornment, "garland," or crown of flowers, for your head and a "pendant" for your neck.

Verses 10-19 offer stern warnings against getting involved with criminals. The language is certainly relevant to the upbringing of children in this society, as well as that of the writer's day. It cannot be assumed that just because a young person has godly parents and a good home he or she will not fall into bad, even criminal companionship. "If sinners entice you" is a dramatic and vivid way of describing how innocent people fall into evil company. How often has that story been enacted! Notice that these criminal elements have such slight regard for the lives, not just the property, of their victims that they actually relish the thought of being able to kill their victims (vv. 11-12). Their crime is wanton, without cause or reason. These criminals entice the innocent with the offer of both easy wealth (v. 13) and real companionship (v. 14), saying, in effect, "Come, we shall make you wealthy, and you will also find what it is like to be in a 'true brotherhood of blood,' a kind of Cosa Nostra." That is the significance of having "one purse" (v. 14*b*).

Verses 15-19 are the parents' admonition against such folly. "Do not walk" means both literally what it says and also figuratively means, "do not habitually associate with," "do not be a companion of such people." The figure of going with them along their path is carried further in verses 15-16. The picture is of a bunch of hoodlums rampaging through the streets of a city, running as fast as they can in search of adventure which will cost some innocent person his goods or his life, or both. But what these hoods do not realize is that they are rushing headlong to their own destruction. They are more senseless than a bird which is wary of a net spread out to catch him. If a bird sees a trap being set for him he is too smart to go into it. But these young hooligans set traps for themselves! It is their "own blood" (v. 18) and their "own lives" (v. 18*b*) which are the price of their vile crimes against the innocent. They simply ambush themselves. Verse 19 summarizes the argument. This is the way of all violence. He who lives by the sword dies by the sword.

Wisdom As a Prophetess (1:20-33)

This is the first of several passages in which wisdom is given the personality traits of a lady. (See also 3:15-19; 8:1-36; 9:1-6.) In most cases, it appears that the writer is merely using a figure of speech in assigning ladylike qualities to wisdom, but at least in one poem (8:22-31) it appears that the writer is thinking of wisdom as having personhood, being part of, yet separate from, the Godhead. In this passage wisdom is pictured as a female messenger with an urgent and crucial word which it is imperative for her to deliver. See her as she "cries aloud" (v. 20), shouting to all who come within the sound of her voice, whether in the streets, marketplace, on top of the walls of the city, or at the city gates. All of these places would be likely vantage points to be heard by large numbers of people.

Her message is plain: "How long?" (v. 22). Here the message is addressed to three audiences: "simple ones," the naive and inexperienced; the "scoffers," arrogant know-it-alls whom no one can teach anything because in their own estimation they already know everything, these opinionated and insolent persons; and "fools," the thick, dull-witted persons cited in verse 7. The voice of wisdom pleads, but her pleas fall on deaf ears. They "refused to listen" (v. 24). She reached out her hand in earnest effort to touch their lives, but they did not heed (v. 24b). They ignored advice and reproof (v. 25). How common is that behavior! Now they must accept the consequences which they have brought upon themselves (vv. 26-32). Note the strong words to describe the retribution coming to the wicked who will not heed the word of God through wisdom. "Panic," coming with the suddenness of a storm, and "calamity" like a whirlwind. "Distress and anguish" are awesome predictions. Worst of all, there will be no comfort from wisdom. Now the calling will be from the other side. Once she called them to repent; they ignored her, but now they beg for her help and she will not answer. They spurned her help. Now they will have to eat "the fruit of their way" (v. 31). Truly, the wages of sin is death. They shall be "sated with their own devices" (v. 31b). They will have a stomach-full of their own wickedness. Talk about retribution! To be sick, not only of sin, but sick on the consequences of your own sin! Verses 32-33 capsule and summarize the entire argument about sinners destroying themselves, while those who listen to the voice of wisdom are saved from the dread of evil.

The Blessings of Seeking Wisdom (2:1-22)

This entire chapter is one extended sentence in poetic form, extolling the virtue and blessings of wisdom. It begins with an admonition to seek wisdom and understanding, then gives five reasons why such a search will be richly rewarded. That is, wisdom bestows five separate blessings upon those who pursue her diligently. It is not by accident that this poem contains exactly twenty-two verses, the number of letters in the Hebrew alphabet.

Verses 1-4 are an introductory appeal to the youthful student to seek wisdom. Two prerequisites are suggested. One is openness. One needs an "ear attentive" and an "inclining heart" to be able to receive God's gift of wisdom. You have to want it before God can give it to you. Second, you have to want it badly. The person who wants wisdom must "cry out," "raise your voice," "seek [wisdom] like silver," "search as for hidden treasures." The words remind us of what Jesus taught about prayer (see Luke 11:5-9; 18:1-8). In the first chapter wisdom is pictured as crying out to people, but here the one desiring her is told to cry to her, for she has much to give, The message is: If you really want it you can have it.

The first of the five blessings of wisdom is that with her comes the true knowledge of God (vv. 5-8). Notice that verse 5 is a variation of the theme of the Book of Proverbs (1:7). Reverence of the Lord is the doorway to knowledge of God, and knowledge of God is the ultimate human blessedness. Who gives wisdom? God gives it. Wisdom is not a human achievement, although to receive it we must really want it, as noted just above. Grace is a gift, too, but it is not given to one who has no desire for it and places no value upon it. God will never force himself upon us.

The second benefit of wisdom is found in verses 9-11, in which the keys to understanding life are promised to the seeker for wisdom. Notice that these are enumerated as "righteousness and justice and equity," the same three and in the same order as found in 1:3. "Every good path" indicates that wisdom is the way to go in life.

The third benefit is that wisdom will protect you from the evil devisings of wicked men (vv. 12-15). Such persons are vividly described: "perverted speech . . . ways of darkness, who rejoice in doing evil and delight in the perverseness of evil, men whose paths are crooked, and who are devious." That is a graphic description of evil.

But wisdom also will save the youth from the wiles of the wicked woman (vv. 16-19), and that is the fourth blessing. Note some of her characteristics: "loose, . . . forsakes [her] companion [husband] . . . and forgets the covenant of her God." The last reminds us that marriage is a sacred covenant, not simply with one's partner, but with God.

The fifth blessing (vv. 20-22) is that the youth who seeks wisdom will be established in life, while the wicked are cut off. An interesting parallel may be seen between these verses and Psalm 1, which is a wisdom psalm.

Wisdom's Origin and Her Rewards (3:1-35)

Here is a poem with three parts, each introduced by the salutation, "My son," (vv. 1,11,21), and each salutation introducing some specific admonition concerning wisdom. These are followed by a variety of exhortations concerning the initial admonition. Thus, verse 1 admonishes the young student not to forget his teacher's teachings. They are the essence of life, and obedience to them will lead to long life and prosperity—according to Old Testament thought, the two most evident ways in which we know that the Lord is pleased with us. The difference between the practical, reward-retribution theology of Proverbs and the questioning theology of Job and Ecclesiastes was noted in the Introduction. Does God reward us for obedience, faithfulness, and loyalty (vv. 1,3)? Jesus said, "Your Father who sees in secret will reward you" (Matt. 6:4,18). The issue is how. Long life and abundance are not promised by Jesus. Not even "favor and good repute" (v. 4) in the sight of man is promised. In fact, Jesus warned that fidelity to God would bring the disfavor of men. The question is not, "Are there consequences to our actions?" The question is, "What kinds of consequences come from a particular kind of behavior?" We may safely reply, "Consequences consistent with the behavior." Whatever we sow we reap, not something else.

As the first set of four verses introduces the issue of rewards, the second set of four verses (5-8) sets forth a second admonition and promises the reward of good health for obedience. Verse 5 is one of the most beloved verses in Proverbs. "With all your heart" needs no elaboration. We all know what it means to say, "I love you with all my heart." Jeremiah wrote to the exiles in Babylon that God said, "When you seek me with all your heart, I will be found by you" (Jer. 29:13b-14a). Verse 6 is also a favorite of multitudes of believers. People ask, "How can I know God's will?" This verse reminds us that God will direct our path (our journey through life) if we will acknowledge that he is truly God in all our ways. The reward is healing and renewal (v. 8).

Verses 9-10 form a unit promising material prosperity in return for faithfulness in the stewardship of possessions. It says, "You give to God what is rightfully his, and he will see to it that your labors will prosper."

Even suffering or reversal of any kind is not to be taken as evidence of God's displeasure, but of his love. The greatest reward of wisdom is the capacity to accept hurt and disappointment without becoming bitter at God for putting you through such trials. But, says the Proverbs, this is God's way of teaching (disciplining) us. This is what verses 11-12 say, and they introduce the second part of the poem with the use of the address, "My son."

Notice that in the Revised Standard Version verses 13-18 form a thought unit. They state the reverse side of the claim made in verses 9-10. Wisdom (which, as we have seen above, is to be "in tune" with God and his world) is far better an achievement than wealth without wisdom. Wisdom is here personified as a lady who brings gifts to those who deserve them. In her right hand (the most important being always on the right) she offers long life; in her left, riches and honor. The acme of wisdom's rewards is expressed in verse 18: "She is a tree of life." The figure of the tree of life takes us back to the Garden of Eden and the beginning of man's experience with God.

Verses 19-20 are an important unit, for they identify wisdom as a participant in the creation. The wisdom which gives correct guidance for this life and brings rich rewards to all who embrace her is the same wisdom by which God created the earth and heavens. Is there here some suggestion of a connection between wisdom as a part of God's Being and the concept of "The Word" in John 1? Many who carefully study the Bible think so.

The third and last division of chapter 3 begins with verse 21. Again, "My son," introduces the thought. There are three thoughts expressed in this section: verses 21-26; 27-30; 31-35. The first unit again stresses the desirability of incorporating wisdom into one's life. She is "life for your soul" (v. 22) and provides that "extra" that makes life more than just a bare existence, that is, "adornment for your neck" (v. 22b). She provides security in the daytime, peace in the night, and confidence in the day of catastrophe (vv. 23-26).

One's duty toward one's neighbor is the subject of verses 27-30. This includes scrupulous honesty in neighborly dealings. Do not neglect paying your honest debt to your neighbor, or put him off, saying "Come back tomorrow; I don't have the money today." Don't take advantage of a neighbor's trustworthiness, and don't live in a state of continual uproar with your neighbors. In short, mind your own business, pay your debts, and don't be a troublemaker.

The concluding unit of this long poem on the rewards of wisdom warns against envying the evil person who appears to be getting away with his wickedness (vv. 31-35). In a series of contrasting pictures the condition of the wicked and the righteous are held up side by side. The main idea is that the wicked person is an offense ("abomination," v. 32) to the Lord. God is offended by our sin. On the other hand, "The upright are in his confidence" (v. 32b). God takes them on the inside and shares the secrets of his purpose with them. What a wonderful gift to be able to walk in and out of God's "White House" as one who is accepted as an intimate friend! Verse 34 emphasizes God's justice. This is a tit for tat form of religion which falls short of Jesus' view that God makes the sun shine upon the just and the unjust. Nevertheless, there is something in life that "pays us back" for the way we live. What we get is what we have given. The words we shout into the canyon come echoing back to us with the same tone of hatred or love.

The Two Ways of Life (4:1-27)

Chapter 4 also has three divisions, each introduced by the address, "My son." It is as though the teacher (or father) is saying "Now, hear this," or "Let me have your attention, please." In the first unit (vv. 1-9) a rationale for this manner of instruction is given. The teacher (or father) was taught by his father; he has therefore a moral responsibility to pass on the moral inheritance which his own father gave him. Here is a lovely picture of the value of moral instruction from one generation to another. Contrary to much popular opinion which argues that children should not be burdened with the values of their parents, the Bible recognizes the moral obligation of the present generation to teach the on-coming one.

Unit 2 of this poem is in verses 10-19. It is strikingly similar in thought to Psalm 1, and it comprises the heart of chapter 4. Consider, the poet says, that there are two ways of life: the way of righteousness and integrity, and the path of the wicked. Walk in the straight and narrow path (see Matt. 7:13-14) and you will have no cause for fear, and no reason to stumble. But when you get off the straight and narrow and begin to explore the ways of wickedness, you get in trouble. So when you come to the inviting sideroad that leads down into evil, do not take it; "pass on" (v. 15). Those who walk the path of evil are described in verses 16-17 as being restless to commit violence against the innocent, and especially of being eager to enlist recruits in evildoing.

The third unit of this poem begins in verse 20, where again the youthful learner's attention is drawn to his teacher's words of wisdom. Verse 23 is a favorite (see Mark 7:14-23) proverb. "[Guard] your heart," for the heart is that organ which controls all of your activities. It is the command post of the human life, and from it go out the orders which the body carries out, whether to do good or evil. If the heart is right, the body will do right.

Verses 25-27 return to the figure of walking in the straight and narrow way. "Watch where you are going" (v. 26, AT), and "Do not swerve to the right or left" (v. 27) like a drunken driver weaving all over the road. Keep your eye on the road and drive on the right side of the road, and you will be doing what you should do as a motorist.

Discourse on the Virtues of Monogamy (5:1-23)

In this day of easy come and easy go in marriage, when "serial monogamy," which is a polite expression for having several legal spouses in one lifetime through the convenience of divorce, is in vogue, it is all the more important that people who believe the Bible should read Proverbs 5:1-23. The poem begins with the customary words of address to get attention, "My son, listen, pay attention" (AT). First he asks for attention; then he gives the teaching.

The problem of sexual immorality must have been also a serious one in the days of the writing of Proverbs, because it is a frequent subject for admonition (see Prov. 2:16-19; 5:1-23; 6:20-35; 7:1-27; 9:13-18). In this poem there is first a general statement of the enticing ways of the "loose" (see also 2:16; 5:20; 7:5) woman. The use of the word "loose" to describe a woman who is not averse to passing out sexual favors to various and sundry men is most appropriate. The Hebrew word here literally means *strange*, suggesting a foreign woman, but it is likely that the writer intends to emphasize that such a woman does not properly belong to the man with whom she is having sex.

Note the intensity of her enticement. Her lips "drip honey," she is so sweet and alluring, and her speech is smoother than the soothing olive oil is to the skin (v. 3). But the end of such irresistible charm is bitter as gall and sharper than a two-edged sword (v. 4). In a change of figure, she leads her victims down what appears to be the primrose path but is really the road to death (v. 5). She is a silly temptress who is on the way to destruction herself and is leading gullible men along with her (v. 6).

Verses 7-14 are a graphic, stern warning expressed in terms of consequences for becoming involved with a woman without morals. First, you give up your honor (v. 9). How many men have made fools of themselves and thrown away the respect of their community over a foolish infatuation! Second, you give your wealth to strangers (v. 10). Do you know any man who has become involved with some predatory female who dangles her body before his eyes, lures him away from his family— then proceeds to "take him to the cleaners" financially or persuades him to change his will to deprive his family of what really belongs to them? Third, at the end you realize that you have made a fool of yourself (vv. 11-14). All the warnings were to no avail. You paid no attention, and now it is too late. Such is the sad story of many a man.

Verses 15-23 extol the virtues of fidelity in marriage. The imagery of drinking from your own cistern, water from your own well (v. 15), is beautiful. Marital love is intended to be a nurturing and refreshing experience. The Revised Standard Version puts verse 16 into the form of a question, although the Hebrew text is not clear at this point. The figure of speech in the verse seems to suggest that of the husband or wife going about all over town passing out the precious water of their sexual love to whoever wants it. Such precious possessions are not to be given to strangers but are reserved for your own private covenant partner (v. 17).

In verses 18-19 we find a beautiful description of the proper place for sensuality in married love. Just because a woman is a wife she need not be unlovely and undesirable. On the contrary, look upon your wife's beauty and enjoy her sensually. Sexual excitement is not a vice when it is expressed within the sacredness of the marriage covenant. "Affection" in verse 19b is a translation for the word *breast*, which word was used by the writer to show that he is not recommending a life of asceticism or marital relationships only for the purpose of procreation. The language is thoroughly consistent with the Bible's healthy view of sexuality within the sacred bounds of marriage.

Verses 20-23 conclude the lecture on marital fidelity by returning to the warning with which it began. Note verse 21. You may suppose that you can get away with sneaking around and being unfaithful to your spouse, but although you might fool your mate and fool the public, you can't fool God. "He watches all his paths," those that go to your door and those that go to the door of the paramour.

Four Short Poems About Rash Promises, Laziness, Perversity and Bad Character (6:1-19)

"Think before you speak" is a proverb among us. Another way of expressing it is, "Connect your tongue to your brain." In verses 1-5 we have such a warning about the hazards of thoughtless and ill-considered promises. To the Hebrew way of thinking, speech was very important. Words spoken could not be recalled; it was as though they had a separate existence of their own when released from someone's mouth. Jesus said that on the day of judgment people would give account for every idle word they utter (Matt. 12:36). Do not go around making rash promies you can't keep, or statements you can't back up with evidence. Such behavior can get you into a lot of trouble.

Notice the down-to-earth quality of the advice in verses 6-11. In this day the so-called "work ethic" is often ridiculed and blamed for many of the ills of society. Those "hung up" on working hard and trying to achieve are regarded by many as the enemies of society where it is quite acceptable to be a consumer rather than a producer, a user instead of a creator. Here the busy little ant is cited as proper example for the lazy person. Watch her as she appears to scurry tirelessly to and fro, ceaselessly doing her work. She is laying in her stores for the rainy days ahead. Verses 9-11 are a wonderful observation about life. Here is the perfect proverb. It expresses a commonly-accepted truth and puts it in graphic, rememberable words. This particular gem of truth is that one does not have to set out deliberately to be trifling and no-account. All one has to do is fold one's hands and let it happen. Life is a lot like gardening. You don't have to plant weeds; all you have to do about them is nothing. They will take over. Inertia is a powerful negative force against which one must struggle.

The picture drawn in verses 12-15 is of the sly, unprincipled, suggestive person who goes about sowing discord, taking delight in dropping veiled, dark hints about life in general or particular persons. This person is deliberately malicious. He has a "crooked mouth," which is the literal translation of verse 12*b*. He does not talk straightforwardly. Everything this person says has an angle, a perverse purpose. Avoid such a person. He is dangerously destructive.

The concluding section of this poem of warnings summarizes, by use of the numerical proverb (see Introduction), the characteristics which God dislikes. Notice the physical imagery of these vices. Five of them are associated with parts of the body: eyes, tongue, hands, heart, feet. The body itself is not evil, no part of it. The use one makes of it, however, is the crucial issue. The body is a temple of the Holy Spirit if we make it so, or it is a vile cesspool if we choose to make it so.

A Long Poem Warning Against Adultery (6:20 to 7:27)

Notice that this poem begins with the familiar address, "My son." This is followed by the usual admonition to follow the guidance of parents, giving a general promise of the benefits of following such guidance (vv. 20-23). Look at the imagery of wisdom's companionship: she will walk with you in the day, watch over you in the night when you sleep, and talk with you as a companion when you are awake. The specific warning of this passage is introduced at verse 24. Wisdom will be a shield for you against "the smooth tongue of the adventuress," literally, the "strange woman."

One reading Proverbs will be impressed with the extensive treatment of the sin of sexual immorality, especially with another man's wife. Remember that these teachings are directed to male youths. There the warnings are to young men, rather than to both sexes, and are designed to caution the inexperienced young man against the wiles of an older married woman who is looking for sexual adventure with a young man. The emphatic teaching is that such sin may not be excused on the ground of temptation to give in to a physical need, but that the sin is folly, a folly that has dire consequences. Thus, "do not let her capture you with her eyelashes" is a graphic metaphor to describe the elaborately made-up temptress who is not only unveiled but made more alluring by the use of cosmetics (v. 25). The lustful looks of such a woman are most enticing to the inexperienced male.

Verse 26 suggests that the adulteress is a woman more greatly to be feared than a prostitute who sells her body for money. The prostitute does it for a loaf of bread, but the stakes are the life of the gullible youth who is ensnared by the sex-hungry adulteress. Retribution is inevitable, says the Proverbs. One does not carry fire in his arms without burning his clothes, or walk on hot coals without burning his feet (vv. 27-28). Just as inevitable is the foolish youth who engages in sex with his neighbor's wife (v. 29). The argument that the guilty persons involved in this immoral sexual act should be excused because they had unmet needs is unacceptable. You don't acquit a thief simply because he argues that he stole to satisfy his hunger (v. 30). Nor will the guilty offender be excused by the outraged husband of the woman who has engaged the youth in this sin. Wounds, dishonor, disgrace, revenge (vv. 33-34) are the words to describe what follows the adultery when it is discovered by the woman's husband. He will not be appeased; though you try to buy him off with gifts, he will not be content (v. 35).

Chapter 7:1-5 reintroduces the subject of the folly and destructiveness of adultery. Notice the similarity between this introduction and 6:20-24. Following the introduction there is a vivid description of the seduction of a young man by an unprincipled married woman (vv. 6-23), and then the lesson is concluded by a familiar warning (vv. 24-27).

In language alive with word pictures, the writer then proceeds to describe a night scene along a city street where he sees a clandestine meeting take place between a man's wife and a simple, inexperienced youth (*pethi*, see 1:4). This foolish young man may not be altogether innocent, for he is "strolling in the direction of her house" (AB) when he encounters the tempress, wife of an absent husband (v. 8). Also it is just as the day ends, that in-between time when there are both enough activity in the street not to make the meeting conspicuous and enough darkness to make it difficult to identify the persons involved (v. 9). Notice the fourfold description of the time of day: twilight, evening, night, and darkness. See the progression of nightfall from twilight to darkness. It is a dangerously alluring scene, and the young man is not equal to the task of resisting.

The woman who meets him, though married, is dressed like a harlot. As far as this woman is concerned, the meeting betwen her and the young man is not a coincidence. She has gone out into the street looking for a youth to entice to go to bed with her. Moreover, this is not a one-time occurrence. She is "boisterous and bold" (v. 11a, AB). She does not stay at home like a faithful wife, but she goes out into the street and marketplace trying to pick up a man (v. 12). She is like a tigress crouched to pounce upon the first prey that comes by (v. 12b).

The brazenness of the woman is expressed in the language of verse 13.

She is not a bit coy, but aggressive. She grabs the young man and begins to kiss him (v. 13). He does not break away and run. Instead he listens to her invitation, as between her kisses she makes him an offer he is unable to refuse. First, she explains that she has a huge meal awaiting him at her house. This is due to the fact that she has been to the house of the Lord and offered a sacrifice that day, which meant that she had meat at her house which had to be consumed that day or the next in order to fulfill the vow of the sacrifice (v. 14). Next, she moves on from the enticement of a good, hot, home-cooked meal to the prospect of satisfying that other basic urge of the young man, the desire for sexual gratification. She tells him of the allures of her bedroom and her perfumed bed, titillating him with thoughts of a night of exciting adventure (vv. 16-18). The clinching temptation which leaves the young man powerless to resist is the promise of complete safety. Her husband, she says, is away. He has gone on a lengthy trip and will not return until "full moon." She can promise that the husband will not be home to catch the young man in his wife's arms, because "he took a bag of money" (v. 20), meaning that he planned to be gone so long that he had to have a supply of money to take care of his needs in his absence from home. No doubt this adulterous adventuress had calculated the number of nights he would be away, and had resolved to have herself a wild time.

Verse 21 suggests that the young man puts up some resistance, for she persuades him with her seductive talk and "compels" him to go home with her. His resistance broken (Did this silly young man try very hard to resist?), "all at once" (v. 22), he is following her. The teacher watching this street scene from his window nearby must have wanted to call out to the youth, but he probably concluded that it would do no good. But his heart was heavy with awareness of the consequences. In a threefold figure, the teacher spells out the tragic end of that night's escapade. He is an ox led to the slaughter, a stag caught in a trap that has its heart pierced by the hunter's arrow, a bird rushing to its destruction into a snare (vv. 22-23). Whether in verse 22b the text should read "stag" (RSV) or "fool" (KJV) is not certain. The Hebrew word at this place is *fool*, but the context suggests the alternate reading "stag," a similar-sounding Hebrew word to the one translated *fool*. In any event, the sense of the verse is the same, namely, a young man who lets himself be drawn into such a sinful adventure is really walking into a trap that one day will cost him his life.

The lesson against sexual sin with an adulterous woman, taught by way of an unforgettable example, concludes with a summary admonition (vv. 24-27). "And so, my sons," the storyteller and teacher concludes, "listen. Stay away from such a temptress. Don't stray into her paths" (v. 25, AT). You won't be as apt to get into trouble if you stay out of the way of it. Further, the young men are warned that such women do not have just one young lover on their string. Like an old-time gunslinger with a notch on his pistol-handle for every man he has shot, this sort of woman makes a game out of collecting young men. She has "laid low" many a victim; her conquests would make up a mighty host (v. 26). And the eventual outcome of involvement with her is the death of her victims. One may say as a Christian that the harshness of the description of consequences leaves out the New Testament concept of forgiveness and restoration. However, such exception should not be noted as a way of discounting the gravity of this offense against God's ordained plan for the home and family.

The Role of Wisdom in Creation (8:1-36)

Chapter 8 is one of the most profound poems in the Book of Proverbs. It consists of three units (vv. 1-11,12-21,22-31) and a closing exhortation (32-36). Each of the three units has twenty-two lines (Unit 2 has twenty-two lines only in the Greek translation called the Septuagint), matching the twenty-two letters in the Hebrew alphabet. The concluding exhortation is composed of eleven lines. Such careful construction of the poem suggests the work of a master craftsman.

However, far more significant than the structure of the poem is its content. Here wisdom is depicted as having a personal existence of her own. As in 1:20-33, wisdom is the speaker as though she were a woman addressing her subjects. Wisdom calls out (8:1,4) from the places of meeting and passings of persons in the streets and gates of a city. See her as she takes her stand in some prominent place and cries out to all who pass her: "Listen to me. I tell you [good] noble things" (v. 6). "I speak the truth, not the abomination of lies" (v. 7, AT). Her words are not "twisted or crooked" (v. 8). To those wanting to do right the words which wisdom speaks are "up front" ("straight," v. 9a). As we say in our colloquial speech, "I want to be 'up front' about this." Then the value of wisdom is compared to precious metals of gold and silver, or to the finest jewels. Nothing, in fact, is comparable with her (v. 11), not even the totality of all people commonly desire.

Verses 12-21 describe Wisdom as a queenly lady with majestic power and authority, ruling the established order of governments through kings, princes, and nobles whom Wisdom elevates to their positions (vv. 15-16). This poetic unit begins in verse 12 with Wisdom's self-description. She "dwell[s] in prudence," which in Hebrew has the meaning of common sense, the ability to avoid foolish mistakes. "Discretion" ("witty inventions," KJV) means intelligent and purposeful planning, or as we might say, "the ability to be decisive, to be a good administrator."

Note that verse 13 restates the theme of the Book of Proverbs (see 1:7), except it states it in reverse: "The fear of the Lord is hatred of evil." Wisdom hates all forms of evil (v. 13b), therefore she will honor and endow with success and wealth those who do not do evil and seek wisdom instead (vv. 17-21). Wisdom loves those who love her and, inasmuch as she is righteous and just, she rewards those who honor her. The pragmatic, tit for tat, reward system suggested here is consistent with the Book of Proverbs. One does not find in this book any suggestion that some persons may try to serve God faithfully but still have poverty and want as their daily companions. No, if you walk with Queen Wisdom you are promised wealth and a full treasury (v. 21).

The third unit (vv. 22-31) of this poem about Wisdom as a female person is by far the most thought-provoking. Scholars do not agree about the meaning of this passage. It could have far-reaching implications for our Christian understanding of Christ as the preexistent Son of God. The issues are twofold. First, does this passage mean to suggest that Wisdom is to be identified as having personality, and therefore in this context should be spelled with a capital "W?" Or is wisdom only meant to be taken as an attribute, although an important one, of God? In other words, is the writer of Proverbs saying, "As God is righteous and just, so is he also the essence of wisdom"?

This commentator believes that something more than an attribute of God's nature is indicated in verses 22-31. Wisdom is here personified, spoken of as present at and the agent of God in creation. This interpretation is based upon the conviction that there is a connection between the idea advanced here and the crucial passages in the New Testament which speak of the eternal preexistent Christ. Read John 1:1-3. "In the beginning was the [Logos] Word. . . . all things were made through him, and without him was not anything made that was made." Paul, in 1 Corinthians 1:24, refers to Christ as "the wisdom of God." In Colossians 1:15-16 Paul writes of Christ as "the image of the invisible God, the first-born of all creation; for in him all things were created." And Hebrews 1:2 describes the eternal Christ as the one "through whom also he [God] created the world." Is there any connection between the Wisdom of verses 22-31 and the Christ of the New Testament? I believe that there is, that the passage in Proverbs is a foregleam of the New Testament doctrine of the preexistent Christ.

The second issue involved in this passage has to do with the role of Wisdom in creation. Remember, if this apparent giving to wisdom the characteristics of personality is only a figure of speech, all that is being said here is a poetic commentary on God's creative activity. But if Wisdom is a person, as Christ is a person, then the work of Wisdom in creation is crucial. Verse 22 is pivotal. "The Lord created me," or as the KJV puts it, "The Lord possessed me." Either of these translations is possible. In this case, the KJV seems better to this commentator because it supports the idea of the eternal and personal nature of Wisdom. Verses 24-25 both indicate, on the other hand, that Wisdom had a beginning point, albeit before anything else came forth from God. "I was brought forth" is an expression for birth. Wisdom, then, is said to have been "born" before God had "birthed" anything else.

Verses 26-31 beautifully describe the presence and companionship of Wisdom in God's mighty works of creation. The thoughtful Bible student will enjoy comparing these poetic expressions with those of Genesis 1 and Job 38. In these verses Wisdom is depicted as God's agent of and witness to the entire creation. Note verse 30 especially. "Then I was beside him, like a master workman." Another reading than "master workman" is "little child." The RSV reading of this Hebrew expression appears better and more fitting to the context of the passage. Whether one identifies wisdom with a lowercase "w" or a capital "W," it is evident that the Proverbs exalt wisdom to a place right next to God himself.

The closing exhortation (vv. 32-36) urges youths who are being instructed to pay attention to wisdom's claims so that they may enjoy a happy, meaningful life. Note especially verse 35a: "For he who finds me finds life." Jesus said that about himself. There is a way to life and a way to death. "All who hate me love death," says wisdom (v. 36b).

Queen Wisdom Versus Dame Folly (9:1-18)

Chapter 9 describes wisdom and folly as though they were two women vying for the attention of youthful passersby. Each has set up her house (vv. 1,14). The "seven pillars" of 9:1 are subject to all kinds of allegorical interpretations, inasmuch as the number seven is so important in the Bible, but the reference here may be only to the pillars that ordinarily surrounded the courtyard of a fine house. In any event, here is a beautiful parable of a feast to which the "simple" (v. 4), that is, the untrained and unsophisticated, are all invited. This passage reminds us of Jesus' parable of the wedding feast as recorded in Matthew 22:1-14. The invitation is sincere and urgent. Queen Wisdom's maids are sent forth to call "from the highest places in the town" (v. 3), "Whoever is unlearned and innocent, Come to the house of Queen Wisdom. She has a feast prepared for you" (vv. 4-5, AT). There is a note of desperation in the invitation: "Leave simpleness and live" (v. 6). To ignore the invitation is to invite death upon oneself.

Verses 7-12 comprise a group of short, pithy maxims, as though these might be samples, tidbits, handed out to entice the invited guests to come on to the banquet in Queen Wisdom's house. The implication is that some will scoff, and those who do so probably cannot be helped by anyone. Trying to correct the scoffer only causes him to abuse the one who would help him (vv. 7-8). On the other hand, the wiser one is the more one will appreciate the opportunity to increase in wisdom (v. 9). Noteworthy is the fact that in this verse the "wise man" and the "righteous man" are equated, as if they are one and the same person. This is not unusual in Proverbs.

Verse 10 strikes again the theme note of the entire book. To be in awe of the Lord is the beginning point, the first principle of wisdom. The last of the proverbs in this series inserted between the pictures of Queen Wisdom and Dame Folly is verse 12. This verse holds that we are individually accountable for the rewards or consequences of our wisdom or folly. It is for ourselves that we are wise (v. 12a), and it is to ourselves that we do damage if we are scoffers, *letz*, one of the Hebrew words in this book which are frequently translated *fool* (12b).

Notice next that Dame Folly is pictured as a harlot, "wanton" and knowing no "shame" (v. 13). She is "noisy," the same word used to describe the wicked woman of Proverbs 7:11. She does not send her servants out to invite young men in (see above the action of Wisdom), but she goes out and seeks to entice them herself. She sits in the door of her house or even makes bold to occupy the public places of the town and calls out to passersby. She copies the invitation of Wisdom (see v. 4), but her meanings are far from the same. She entices them with the invitation to drink "stolen water," a thinly-veiled reference to illicit love, as is also the reference to "bread eaten in secret" (v. 17). The irresistibility of clandestine wrongdoing is a force all of us have to grapple with. The awesome tragedy of this picture is the conclusion. The simpleton accepts the enticement of the temptress to come to her house, and he has no awareness that he is entering the house of death (v. 18). Queen Wisdom says, "Come to me and live" (v. 6, AT). Dame Folly says, "Come to me and die" (v. 18, AT). This is life's basic choice.

Book II

10:1 to 22:16

Chapter 10:1-32

At 10:1 the second "book " of this collection of wise sayings begins. As noted above, chapters 1—9 consist of a collection of poems of varying length extolling the virtues of wisdom while warning against the destructiveness of folly. When we come to 10:1 we note a clear change of style in the writing. The proverbs of 10:1 to 22:16 are almost all two-line maxims assembled for the most part without any logical sequence. For this reason it is impossible to make an outline of this section of the book. This collection is entitled, "The proverbs of Solomon" (v. 1), and is generally believed to be the oldest section of the entire book. Inasmuch as Solomon is considered the patron of Old Testament wisdom, these proverbs likely originated in his time. Most of the proverbs of Part II are two-line antithetical observations, the two lines connected by the conjunction "but." The very first proverb in the collection, 10:1, is a classic example. It emphasizes the prime place of the home in teaching children, and also contrasts the gladness brought on by a wise son with the heartbreak that comes from having a foolish one. The maxim reminds us that there is no success a parent can enjoy that will compensate for the grief of failing with one's child.

Verse 2 reflects the conviction of the Proverbs that right living pays off, whereas wickedness, though it seems to bring prosperity, actually is not profitable. Verse 3 is a variation of the same reward-retribution theme, arguing that the Lord will take care of the righteous but will block the cravings of the wicked. In other words, God will always be found on the side of the upright. The promise that the Lord does not let the righteous go hungry (v. 3a) would be a difficult one if one were starving. Verse 4 reflects the same prudential view of life, as it is claimed that poverty is the result of "a slack hand," or laziness, while wealth is the result of diligence. One might want to say that there is surely a connection between these causes and effects, but it would be erroneous to absolutize the claim. Verse 5 simply reinforces the same teaching, namely, that if one works hard one will prosper but if one "sleeps in harvest" one brings shame upon one's family.

In every case an argument is made for the workability of life to the advantage of those who are wise and righteous. God works things out for those who by their wisdom and righteousness (seen by the Proverbs to be two sides of the same thing) prove to be worthy of his confidence. The consequences of righteousness or wickedness continue even after death, although Proverbs has no conception that personal life may continue beyond the grave. The consequences, as stated in verse 7, are that the memory of the righteous will live on after him, while that of the wicked person will decay and rot and disappear.

In verse 10 the expression "He who winks the eye" is a vivid figure of speech to describe malicious deception. Can you see this conniving fellow who lies to you while assuring you that he is giving you the true story? Avoid such a person. Verse 12 should be engraved on tablets of stone and placed in the center of the table wherever heads of state meet to discuss international problems. "Hatred stirs up strife,/but love covers all offenses." Love overlooks others' faults. Read 1 Corinthians 13.

Verse 15 again shows the commitment of Proverbs to the doctrine of wealth as a blessing and poverty as a curse. It makes the observation, which unfortunately is true in most cases, that there are many advantages to having money, and many hazards to being without it. We may talk self-righteously about honest poverty, but the poor know that it is not all that much of a blessing.

Verse 16, concerning the wages of the righteous and the gain of the wicked, reminds the Christian of Romans 6:23, and makes one wonder if Paul had this proverb in mind when he wrote that verse.

Verse 18 stands out in this collection because it is not antithetic, but synthetic or progressive (see Introduction). It says that if you hate and pretend that you do not, you have lying lips, and that if you slander another you are a fool. In either case, truth-telling is the best policy. Verse

19 is also about speaking. It says that a lot of talk is likely to be an attempt to cover up for wrongdoing. Remember one of our own contemporary maxims: "The more a man proclaims his honesty the more carefully you had better watch your wallet."

Verse 21 says that the righteous person is a source of sustenance for many, while the fool (wicked) cannot even sustain himself. Verse 23 points out that there are "different strokes for different folks," to use another American aphorism. It is the fool's sport to do wrong. He actually enjoys trying to get away with something. On the other hand, it is the righteous person's pleasure to do right. Another verse that emphasizes consequences is verse 24. The contrast is highlighted by the words "dreads" and "desire." Each person gets what he deserves from what he has done.

Verse 26 has a humorous note in it. As irritating as vinegar to one's teeth, and smoke to the eyes, is a lazy person to those who are trying to get some work out of him. The remaining verses of chapter 10 all reinforce the basic teaching of Proverbs, that righteousness or wisdom will bring forth the Lord's blessing, while wickedness or folly will produce destruction. The Proverbs is confident about reward for goodness and punishment for evil.

Chapter 11:1-31

Verse 1 of this chapter exhorts the young men who are learning these proverbs to be honest in business, not cheating customers with a "false balance." Similar admonitions are found in 16:11; 20:10,23. Morality is not theoretical; it gets down to practical issues such as giving honest weight when you measure out the wheat you are selling.

Pride is condemned and humility praised in numerous proverbs, including 11:2; 13:10; 15:33; 16:18-19; 18:12; 22:4. In 11:2 pride is seen as the prelude to disgrace.

Money is not everything, says 11:4. This is a bit surprising, in view of the high value placed upon wealth as evidence of the Lord's pleasure with the person who is wealthy. But "in the day of wrath," perhaps a time of calamity, money cannot purchase deliverance. Only an upright life is adequate coin for that transaction. Verse 8 plays the familiar theme of the contrast between the condition of the righteous and the wicked, while verse 9 decries slander and malicious gossip. Verse 10 reflects the social value of righteousness, for when the righteous prosper the entire city is helped and thus rejoices, while when the wicked perish the city is glad because it is delivered from the wicked's oppressiveness. Verse 11 continues the theme of the city and its blessing or curse from the righteous or the wicked.

Verse 13 reflects the contemptuousness in which gossip and talebearing are held by the Proverbs. Verse 15 is a two-line proverb that summarizes the teaching of 6:1-5, a warning against putting oneself in another's power by obligating oneself to the other's debts. Verse 17 makes the observation that kindness not only helps others, but is a benefit to oneself, while the opposite is true of cruelty. When you try to hurt somebody else you end up hurting yourself. In verse 18 there is yet another contrast between the ways of wickedness and righteousness. The wicked man "earns deceptive wages," that is, he gets what he works for, and what he gets is counterfeit money, while the righteous person receives a genuine reward. Verse 21 reminds us that the laws of retribution are inescapable. "Be assured" means literally "You can shake hands on it," like men sealing an agreement, saying, "That's it, the matter is settled." So God says we can count on evil being punished.

Verse 22 is an earthy, humorous observation about the inappropriateness of crude behavior on the part of a woman. It is as out of place and as incongruous as a lady's gold nose-ring (such rings were considered beautiful accessories to a lady's dress) put in a pig's snout!

Verses 24-28 comprise a series of aphorisms about the virtue of using material resources generously. Once again the truth is presented in contrasting life-styles. One man is generous in giving, yet he always seems to have enough for all his own needs. Is this merely a coincidence? The wise do not think so. It is God's doing. Another man stingily holds back what his religious and moral duty obligates him to give, but rather than having more for himself he seems always not to have enough. His condition is no more coincidental than the other. Verse 25 is a synonymous statement (both lines saying the same thing) expanding upon the first line of the preceding statement about the generous person. Verse 26 is a further comment on the claim of verse 24. Here the reference is to the merchant who corners the grain market in a village and then holds it back until the price goes up and he can make an exorbitant profit. We call it being a smart businessman, but the Bible considers it a form of sinful greed and exploitation of the helpless. Verse 28 summarizes this group of observations about the use and misuse of money by predicting the downfall of the person who puts his trust in money. It should be remembered that the wise did not consider wealth in itself to be evil. In fact, the possession of wealth indicated to them that God was pleased with the possessor of wealth. However, if one became haughty, proud, and greedy, and began to make money an idol, the blessing would become a curse.

Verse 30 is difficult. Comparing the King James Version with the Revised Standard Version will disclose an entirely different interpretation of the meaning of the second line. In the first line the "tree of life" presents no problem, as it is a metaphor calling up the symbolism of Genesis 2 and the Garden of Eden. But in the second line the King James Version understands the words to mean that wisdom draws the souls of people to herself. The problem with this interpretation (all translation is interpretation) is that it overlooks the fact that the word translated "winneth" always means *destroys* in Hebrew. Therefore the Revised Standard Version translators followed an early Greek translation of this passage in reading "lawlessness" in place of "wise." Verse 31 concludes this chapter with the observation that reward for the righteous and retribution for the wicked are both certain to happen in this life. Inasmuch as there is little evidence of belief in life after death in this period, the assurance of a just outcome would have to be within the bounds of this earthly life.

Chapter 12:1-28

The succession of two-line observations about the contrasts in the behavior of the righteous and the wicked and their consequences continues in this chapter. As noted above, it is difficult to establish any sequential pattern to the proverbs, although it should be noted that verses 13-19 all relate in some way or other to speaking.

Verse 1 declares that there are no shortcuts to learning. One must pay the price of discipline. The basic meaning of discipline is teaching, not punishment, but the necessity to endure some discomfort and stress as a condition of learning is implicit in the word. Things worth having do not come free, including wisdom.

Verse 4 requires no explanation, but it is cited for its classic statement of the paternal nature of the Old Testament. A wife is either the best or the worst thing a husband can have. In biblical times, she was regarded as his possession, and if he had a good wife he was most fortunate; if bad, a wife could be a terrible burden.

Whereas most of the proverbs of this longest section of the book (10:1 to 22:16) are antithetical, stating opposite sides of a truth, a few are comparative, "better this than that," proverbs. Such a one is 12:9. This proverb extols the virtue of one who makes an honest living even though he may be lightly esteemed by self-important persons who put on a big show but don't have two nickels to rub together. The RSV rendering of the Hebrew text, "works for himself," is to be preferred to the KJV wording, "hath a servant." The next two proverbs, verses 10-11, are related to the praise of honest and humble toil. Verse 10 holds that a good man is concerned for the life of his beast of burden, his ox or ass, and verse 11 says that the same kind of man will work hard and take care of his land. The down-to-earth quality of Proverbs is always impressive.

It has been noted that verses 13-19 are in some way all related to the issue of the importance of speech. By our words we either "trip ourselves up with a slip of the tongue," or else we bless others and are blessed. Verse 15 may appear not to be related to talking, but it surely reflects the common observation that "you can't tell some people anything because they already know it all." It is the wise person who can learn from others. He believes that everyone can teach him something. Verse 16 advises against being quick-tempered. It won't hurt to suffer insult, Jesus said. Verse 17 reflects a trial scene where the truth speaker gives honest testimony, while the liar perjures himself. The power of words to hurt or heal is the subject of verse 18. Words are like sword thrusts or else like healing balm. Finally, verse 19, truthfulness is enduring, while lying is only temporarily successful. Sooner or later the lies catch up with one. Truth will come out. Verse 22 advances the same argument about falsehood and truth, saying that the Lord finds lying lips abominable but delights in truth saying. Verse 23 is also about knowing when to keep one's mouth shut. The wise man is often silent about what he knows. The fool is just the reverse; he tells everything he knows to everybody he meets.

This chapter is concluded with the basic theme of Proverbs, namely righteousness leads to life. Notice that there is a sharp difference between the King James Version rendering of the second line in verse 28 and the Revised Standard Version. The King James Version makes the proverb synonymous, the second line reinforcing the first, while the RSV understands the second line as antithetical to the first. The problem is that the

Hebrew text is unclear in this verse. However, the truth is quite clear. The way to life is the way of righteousness.

Chapter 13:1-25

Notice that admonitions and observations about the youth listening to the instructions of his elders, particularly his parents, intersperse the proverbs (10:1, 12:1; 13:1). The whole system of education was based upon passing on the lessons of the ages to the succeeding generation. Verses 2-3 speak further of the importance of words. What we say inevitably reflects the kind of persons we are. The same theme is expressed in verse 5, where the wicked man literally "raises a stench" with his talk and his actions. In verse 7 there is a condemnation of two kinds of deception—the poor man who puts on airs and pretends to be rich, and the rich man who "poor mouths" all the time, pretending to be poor. Both are reprehensible.

The Proverbs do not give a blanket endorsement of wealth. Consider verse 11, where wealth too easily attained, perhaps through unscrupulous means, is condemned and judged to be temporary. "Easy come, easy go." But wealth accumulated through hard work has a lasting quality. Many a person has been ruined by getting rich too fast and easily, turning his head and spoiling his values.

Verse 12 is a simple observation about a common human characteristic. Disappointment is hard to take. "Hope deferred," it is called here. On the other hand, a "desire fulfilled" is a source of refreshment, the meaning of the expression "tree of life." But, of course as the writer of this maxim would know, much of the time we are compelled to live with hopes deferred. Paul's words in Romans 5:1-5 are helpful. He says that we can live without total fulfillment of our hope because we already have a foretaste of things to come in the gift of the Holy Spirit in us.

Verses 13-14 commend respect for the teaching and the teacher. The person who despises the lessons of the past dooms himself to repeat its self-destructive errors. Verse 18 has a similar message. Ignore instruction and you invite poverty and disgrace, but heed reproof (We all need reproof because no one is right all the time) and you will gain honor because you will become the kind of person whom others honor. Verse 20 emphasizes a similar truth. "Watch your company," this proverb literally advises. "A person is known by the company he keeps" would be another way of putting it. Associate with wise men and it rubs off on you; go about with fools and you will damage yourself.

Verse 19 logically relates to verse 12. "Hope deferred makes the heart sick" (v. 12), but a "desire fulfilled is sweet to the soul" (v. 19). There appears to be little connection between the two lines of verse 19; each is a declaration quite independent of the other.

Verses 21-22 repeat a favorite theme in Proverbs: the misfortune of the wicked and the prosperity (even to the third generation, v. 22) of the righteous.

Verse 24 is a classic example of the antithetical and paradoxical proverb. The antithesis is presented in the words "hates" (first line) and "loves" (second line). The paradox is in the way love or hate is expressed. Superficially, we would suppose that punishment would indicate lack of love, but the reverse is the truth.

Chapter 14:1-35

This chapter presents numerous textual problems in which translators become involved, resulting at times in wide variations between translations. A comparison of the King James Version and Revised Standard Version translations of verses 1,3,9,14,17,24,32 will illustrate the difficulties encountered in this chapter.

Verse 1, like most of the proverbs of 10:1 to 22:16, is antithetic, expressing opposite sides of a truth. Wisdom is a builder; folly is a destroyer. Wisdom constructs; folly destructs.

In verse 3 the King James Version is a better translation than the Revised Standard Version. "Pride" grows out of the mouth of the fool, like a shoot springing up from the ground. The second line of the couplet seems to fit better with the Revised Standard Version translation.

Verse 5 is an observation about perjury. In a society where the word of a witness might condemn or free the accused, the veracity of the witness is imperative.

Verse 6 says that the scoffer, who is not stupid but has no respect for the Lord, can never gain wisdom no matter how hard he tries. Without fear of the Lord, it is impossible to be wise. With fear of the Lord, wisdom comes easily.

Verse 7 is synonymous, the second line completing the thought of the first. It simply admonishes getting away from a fool as quickly as possible because he won't help you in any way.

Verse 8 reminds us that one of the attributes of wisdom is the ability to weigh the present in terms of consequences in the future. What this is telling us is that the wise person makes good decisions, while the foolish person deceives himself.

"Fools make a mock at sin" (KJV) seems to be a better translation of verse 9 than the Revised Standard Version, although neither follows the wording of the Hebrew text.

Verse 10 is an observation that everyone will endorse. As the old spiritual says, "Nobody knows the trouble I've seen." The deepest feelings of sadness and joy are private. Only the Lord knows (see 15:11; 16:2; 24:12).

The contrast of verse 11 lies in the fact that the "house," which should be sturdy, is less enduring than the "tent," because the first is inhabited by the wicked, while the second is occupied by the righteous. The way of evil looks substantial, while the way of good oftens seems tentative and frail, but in the long run it is the good which endures.

Verse 12 is duplicated in Proverbs 16:25. Its sense is plain: A person can rationalize the course he has chosen, even though it will lead him to ruin and death.

According to verse 13, our experience is always a mixture of joy and sadness. Even in the sound of laughter one who listens carefully can hear the minor notes of sadness. This is not simply a pessimistic reading of life, but a realistic recognition that we move between the two poles of joy and sorrow, pleasure and pain.

Verse 14 in the King James Version reads "backslider." The Hebrew text means "turned away in heart." This is not a reference to apostasy, but to the deliberate choice of the way of evil. Each person—the evil and the righteous—reaps what he sows. This is the standard position taken in the Proverbs.

Verse 15 is a contrast between the gullible, simpleminded person and the discerning person. Prudence is the ability to size things up and make good decisions. Verse 16 is a companion of 15, and simply reverses the previous saying. Where the King James Version reads "confident" the Revised Standard Version has "careless." The Hebrew says that the fool "trusts," that is, he believes anything people tell him, as it says in verse 15. Verse 17 belongs with the preceding two verses, but its meaning is unclear, especially the second line. The overall message is that a person who has a "short fuse," is quick-tempered, will act foolishly. The meaning of the second line is not clear.

Verse 19 is a confident statement of the triumph of good over evil. Although this is frequently stated in the Proverbs, Job and Ecclesiastes contest the claim.

Verses 20-21 are both statements about neighborliness. In the first it is observed that the poor person is disliked (disdained) even by his neighbors, while the second chastises those who dislike their poor neighbors. It is easy to fawn over the rich (v. 20b), but real happiness comes from being kind to the poor (v. 21b). Read Luke 14:12-14 for Jesus' view of this matter.

Verse 22 states a truth in the form of a question, a rarity in Proverbs, but the intent is only to emphasize the certainty of the matter about which the question is asked. The answer expected is an unqualified yes.

Work, not words, is the way to productivity. Don't just talk about how busy you are, get busy and turn out some results. This is the meaning of verse 23.

Verse 24 seems more accurately translated in the King James Version than in the Revised Standard Version. It is consistent with the view of Proverbs that wealth is the just reward ("crown") of wisdom.

Verse 25 reflects the absolute importance of having a truthful witness where someone is accused of a crime in which a guilty verdict would cost him his life. In such a case, a liar is not just an annoying person; he is a traitor.

Verses 26-27 are both about "fear of the Lord," which is at the heart of Proverbs' understanding of wisdom. In reverence for the Lord there is security for oneself and one's family, and there is also the source of life.

Verse 28 makes the simple observation that a king without subjects is no king at all, but a laughingstock.

Verses 29 and 30 are parallels, each commending the virtue of tranquility and even-temperedness. "Slow to anger" is in Hebrew "long of nostrils," while quick-temperedness is "short of nostrils," referring to the fact of quiet breathing when calm, snorting when angry.

Verse 31 expresses a deep social concern for the poor. This is remarkable in light of the fact that poverty was often judged by the wise to be evidence of God's displeasure with the person who was poor. Here, however, it is recognized that whoever oppresses the poor person has insulted his Creator, while being kind to the poor is a way of honoring God. Jesus said, "As you did it to one of the least of these my brethren, you did it to me" (Matt. 25:40).

Verse 32 marks another textual problem, reflected in the variations between the King James Version and Revised Standard Version. Does the righteous have "hope in his death" (KJV), or is his hope in his integrity? The former is what the Hebrew text reads, but the suggestion that the righteous might have some expectation of life after death is not consistent with the standard position of Proverbs that death brings one to Sheol, the place of nothingness. Therefore, the Revised Standard Version translators followed the readings of early Greek and Syriac translations.

The meaning of verse 33 is that in the case of either wisdom or folly the appropriate character is permanently displayed. The wise person acts wisely, and the fool acts like a fool. Both are in character.

Verse 34 is a well-known motto which ought to be engraved on the walls of all legislative halls where people acknowledge that God is rightful sovereign of the state. Sin is a "reproach," a producer of want. Sin is not merely a rebuke; it is a scandal.

Verse 35 is a proverb which suggests that the king is dependably beneficent. Read Romans 13:1-6.

Chapter 15:1-33

It has been observed that speech (the tongue or lips) is an important item on the list of crucial behaviors taught in Proverbs. By lying talk another may lose his life; by reckless, careless talk great harm may be done; by foolish talk we reveal ourselves as foolish; by careful, guarded speech, or by silence, we may show our wisdom. Notice how many of the proverbs of chapter 15 observe or admonish about wise or foolish speech: 1-2,4,7,23,28. In a day when "talk is cheap" it might be well to reflect upon the importance of words.

Verse 1 is familiar. Gentleness in response to anger, refusing to respond in like kind, is a virtue to be praised. Paul wrote, "When reviled, we bless" (1 Cor. 4:12b). That is the meaning here. On the other hand, a harsh word (literally, "painful word") merely heightens and accelerates the other's anger. Verse 2 presents a vivid contrast between the style of the wise in speaking and that of the fool. The wise person speaks when he has something useful and helpful to say, while the fool simply runs at the mouth, pouring out in an uncontrolled torrent the foolishness of his idle thoughts.

Verse 3 acknowledges God's omniscience. He sees and knows all. The word to describe God's "keeping watch" is used of a watchman.

In verse 4 the expression "tree of life" is again found, used here as elsewhere to suggest refreshment, like rain on parched earth. A wholesome, "gentle tongue" helps, but a perverse one breaks the spirit of the person who suffers from it. Perverseness is "turning upside down" (AT); it is calling dark, light, or day, night. It is not simply loose talk, but deliberate lying.

Verse 6 is a straightforward claim that righteousness will be rewarded with material prosperity, while evil will produce poverty.

Verses 8-9 tell the reader that the Lord holds as an abomination both the worship and the ways of wicked people. Verse 8 emphasizes worship, first that offered by the wicked and then that offered by the righteous. Verse 9 emphasizes work, or manner of living. Neither worship nor work will please the Lord if they are performed out of a wicked heart.

Verse 11 is a restatement of the truth of verse 3. God, who knows the deepest depths of death and the abyss, certainly has no trouble seeing into the hearts of people.

Verses 13 and 15 are similar comments upon the experience of both joy and sorrow. Note that they not only put the two lines in antithetical relationship, but the two proverbs are antithetical to one another. In the first "a glad heart" comes first, while in the second "the afflicted" are in the first line. Both proverbs not only suggest the obvious, namely, that there is a correlation between what we are experiencing and the way we feel. They also suggest that there is an important correlation between the way we react to life's experiences and the way we either rise or fall. If we put on a cheerful face despite not feeling like it, we make our condition actually better. If we mope about, things seem worse.

Verses 16 and 17 are two interesting comments of comparison, or "better this than that." Verse 16 says that it is better to be poor and love the Lord, holding him in reverence, than it is to be rich but have a lot of trouble. Money is not everything. Verse 17 is on a similar theme. "Dinner of herbs" is certainly a plain, poor person's fare, while "a fatted ox" would be considered the epitome of gourmet feasting, but the contrast between love and hatred makes the difference between the two conditions.

As the tongue is an important subject for the Proverbs, so is the temper. See 14:17,29-30; 17:27; 19:11; 22:24; 26:21; 29:22. A man who easily loses his temper is a source of continual strife, whereas a cool-tempered person calms the waters when they are stirred (v. 18).

Verse 19 may be taken two ways. The road of the lazy man is overgrown with thorns because he does not travel it much, nor does he keep it clean. Or it may simply mean that the sluggard's path is full of obstacles, while the upright's path is a paved road, and things are smooth for his traveling.

Verse 20 strikes a familiar note about the blessing or curse to his parents of a wise or foolish son.

Verse 21 suggests that folly is not mere foolishness but evil, and the man of folly really enjoys doing wrong.

Verse 22 emphasizes the value of counseling. Perhaps this saying was intended to justify the presence of counselors in the court of the king. Whatever its intention, it is good advice. Don't be afraid to ask for help from somebody who knows what he or she is talking about! Verse 23 appears to be the complement of this idea. From the counselor's side, to be able to help another with an appropriate word (a word in season) is a source of gratification. "How good it is!"

Verse 24 is not an observation about heaven and hell, inasmuch as the ancient Hebrews did not entertain the idea of heaven and hell seriously. In fact, in Jesus' time the issue was hotly contested, the Pharisees arguing for resurrection and life after death, the Sadducees disputing it. We as Christians believe in the resurrection and the life everlasting because of the resurrection of Christ the Lord. In verse 24 the argument is that wisdom puts one on the road to life (here and now) and it is an upward road, whereas folly leads to death (Sheol).

Pride and arrogance represent the height of insolent rebellion against the Lord. He opposes the proud, but he defends the defenseless, and none is more defenseless in a male-dominant culture than the widow. That is the meaning of verse 25. Verse 26 states again that God is on the side of the upright (in this verse, "pure" is the person who has kept himself from ritual defilement and is acceptable to come before the altar of God), and opposes the wicked.

Verse 27 suggests that many public officials were tempted by bribes and that such corruption inevitably brought grief to their families. The same law of consequences is in force today. Sooner or later corruption in government comes out.

"Think before you speak," or "Don't substitute many words for deliberate thinking," is a good modern interpretation of verse 28.

Verse 30 is synonymous rather than antithetic. "The light of the eyes" and "good news" correspond. The light is in the eyes of the news bringer. When you see his happy face you take heart because you know he has something good to tell you. Verse 31 follows logically upon the preceding one. It is a synthetic or progressive proverb, that is, the two lines are needed to complete the thought. The theme is familiar in Proverbs: Life does not simply approve of us, it affirms us, often through rebuke. Sometimes the highest form of love is "wholesome admonition," not simply destructive criticism.

The closing two verses of this chapter applaud the hearing of instruction. The student ignores instruction to his own peril, and the supreme lesson to be learned is reverence of the Lord. You have to crawl before you walk, and you have to be humble (teachable) before you merit being honored.

Chapter 16:1-33

Even though the maxims in Proverbs appear often to deal with ordinary, mundane matters, underlying them is the belief that all of life is related to God. Sometimes this is only implied, but in verses 1-7 the belief is explicit. In each verse the Lord is named as the source or controller of people's lives. Thus verse 1 says that even though a man may make big plans that leave the Lord out, God has a way of getting his word said in our lives. Notice that the King James Version has a different interpretation. It says that both the plans of the mind and the words of the mouth originate in God. Verse 2 seems to favor the Revised Standard Version interpretation of verse 1, namely, that man may propose but God disposes. Man may justify whatever he does, but it is God who tests ("weighs") the inmost being of us all.

Verse 3 admonishes trusting the Lord with your work, taking him as a partner in your plans, with the assurance that if you will do so he will assure your success. There is no hocus-pocus in this promise. If your work is peddling dope or engaging in the numbers racket, you ought not to expect the Lord to bless your plans. The confidence that the Lord is in charge of everything that exists is expressed in verse 4. Even the wicked are, in the view of the Proverbs, part of the divine plan. Their purpose is to exist so that God may punish them at the appropriate time.

Arrogance has been previously condemned. See 11:20-21; 13:10. Verse 5 makes another statement about the subject.

Verse 6 expresses a prophetic conception of the means of forgiveness. To have sins atoned for (covered up), one should render the sacrifice of covenant love and fidelity to the Lord. These two ways of offering the sacrifice of oneself to the Lord are called in the King James Version "mercy and truth." The Hebrew words are two of the most important in the Old Testament, particularly the prophets. The first ("loyalty"), often translated *mercy*, means more accurately, covenant love, or loyal love. The second word means faithfulness or fidelity. The words are often put together, for together they express the essence of a deep and abiding relationship. Covenant love keeps fidelity from becoming a binding legalism, while fidelity keeps love from becoming mere sentimentalism. If genuine atonement is a spiritual act of giving oneself to the Lord, so worship is a way of avoiding evil. See Micah 6:8 for a prophetic expression of this idea.

Verse 7 promises that the Lord will deliver a man whose ways please him from his enemies. It is a synthetic or progressive parallelism, the two lines making a complete thought.

Verse 8 is another "better this than that" proverb of comparison. This proverb is very similar to 15:16.

See verse 1 for explanation of verse 9.

Verses 10,12, and 13-15 reflect the exalted place of the king in Israel's wisdom thought. The wise were at first almost certain to have been members of the king's court, and it is not surprising, therefore, that such high regard for kingship is reflected in their writings. The prophets were not so favorably inclined toward kingship (see 1 Sam. 8:10-18; Hosea 8:4; 13:10-11 as examples). Verse 10 ascribes to the king the authority to speak inspired words in decision making. He does not sin when he gives judgment, because he speaks the whole truth. But this is only if the king is a man of God, as verse 12 makes plain. If the king is an evil man it is a worse abomination in the Lord's sight than if he were an ordinary man, because he has so much power. Verse 13 emphasizes the crucial importance of the king being a righteous man, and not a knave. Verses 14-15 stress the king's power. The king's anger (v. 14) is something to be feared. His favor (v. 15) is like the refreshing spring rain in a dry land where rainfall is always a welcome gift to the farmer whose fields are parched. See 25:5 and 29:4 for additional examples of the king's importance to the nation.

Verse 11 reminds us that God is Lord of all, including the systems of weights and balances. Think how indispensable are uniform and dependable measurements, yet how we mindlessly take them for granted. How do you know whether you have received a full pound's worth when you buy a pound of butter, meat, or fruit? How do you know that the pump has delivered ten gallons of gasoline to your tank when the meter reads "10"? We would have chaos if there were no standards of measurement. The ancients had additional problems in commercial transactions. They had not only to be sure that the scales weighing the merchandise were fair, but also that the weights measuring the silver coins, called shekels, were standardized, else the scales might weigh a full shekel short, or a short shekel as full. This verse therefore becomes an excellent illustration of the wise teachers' belief that everything is sacred, and that God is the author of all that is.

Verse 16 is another salutation to wisdom as the highest achievement of a person's life.

Verse 17 uses the metaphor of a journey to describe the manner in which the wise person conducts his life. The road he takes does not pass through Sin City; rather, the righteous person watches his step because he knows that the best way to avoid sin is to stay out of its way as much as possible. "Lead us not into temptation."

Verse 18 is a familiar and commonplace observation about the pitfalls of pride. Haughtiness in the Bible is considered to be an offense against God, for it reflects the desire to be something other than what God made us to be.

Verse 19 reflects the same truth found in 15:16 and 16:8.

Verse 20 is another reference (see 13:13) to the importance of God's Word to the wise. Following the commandments of God is the secret of prosperity and happiness.

Verses 21 and 23 are both synonymous proverbs lauding pleasantness and discernment as assets to the persuasiveness of one's teaching. The teacher-preacher who packages his truths in attractive covers will more likely be heard than one who makes no effort to be pleasant. "You can catch more flies with honey than vinegar."

Verse 22 has a plain lesson to teach about wisdom and folly, but there is an interesting difference between the King James Version and Revised Standard Version translations of the second line. The King James Version says that it is a waste of time to try to teach fools, while the Revised Standard Version says that their folly is their own punishment. Who is the greatest loser when a child refuses to learn in school? The child.

Verse 24 also salutes the value of pleasantness. See verses 21 and 23.

Verse 25 is a duplicate of 14:12.

Verse 26 says simply that the need to eat is a strong motivator to industriousness. If you get hungry enough, you will probably go to work.

Verses 27-30 is a series of synonymous proverbs denouncing evil men, particularly those who do evil by malicious talk. The worthless fellow "digs a hole" to trap others, his speech withering and destroying life like a forest fire (v. 27). He spreads strife like a virus, and enjoys the malicious whisper which alienates close friends. He delights in enticement, taking his more innocent neighbor to dens of iniquity. His gestures are suggestive. As he whispers his lewd suggestions to another, he winks knowingly and makes provocative signs with his mouth (v. 30).

Verse 31 honors old age, it being presumed by the wise that the attainment of advanced years is prima facie evidence that one is righteous. It is assumed that the wicked die prematurely.

Verse 32 praises the virtue of patience and self-control. See 14:29.

Verse 33 graphically declares that people may suppose that what happens is only "the luck of the draw," but that the Lord really makes the choices which come to us. "The lot is cast into the lap" refers to the practice of concealing the lots to be drawn in the fold of one's robe, from which one would then draw a lot.

Chapter 17:1-28

Tranquility in the home was held in high esteem, as verse 1 indicates. To have a happy home life is a great blessing. Continual strife is a curse upon a family, no matter how materially well off it may be. Verse 2 also relates to the household, holding that a wise slave may actually be put in charge of a renegade son, and may even replace him in the father's will, or at least be adopted as one of the sons and thus inherit a son's portion. Israelite law provided that each son received one portion of the father's estate, except the first son, who got a double portion. Daughters did not inherit unless there were no sons, and wives never inherited. Verse 3 is a vivid metaphor about life's trials. As men refine precious metal because they want to purify it of dross, so the Lord subjects his chosen ones to discipline so that they may be pure.

Verse 4 observes that one who is intent upon doing evil is easily persuaded by a wicked person, and a liar will listen to one who uses his mouth to hurt others. We find our own kind of people. "Birds of a feather flock together."

For an interpretation of verse 5 see comment on 14:31.

Most grandparents will say "Amen" to verse 6. This proverb witnesses to the great value placed on the family by the Bible.

"Do not expect excellent, upright speech from a fool, nor lies from the mouth of a prince" (v. 7, AT). The key to this proverb is a play on words between fool *(nabhal)* and prince *(nadhibh)*. This kind of fool is not merely unlearned, simple, or stupid. He is a perverter and a distorter. See Psalm 14:1 for another example of the *nabhal*.

Verse 8 observes that the briber of others believes that his money or his favors will buy whatever he wants. His bribe is like a magic charm, he thinks.

Verse 9 excites the imagination with the wonder and power of the act of forgiveness. If you forgive another an offense against you, you are making a powerful gesture of love. But if you go around telling other people what the other did to you, you are going to create alienation and lose a friend, or a spouse, or an associate. Talk to the offender, not about him, if you want to make it right. Verse 10 fits naturally with the one preceding it, as it reminds us that to rebuke a sensitive person affects him more deeply than a hundred blows would affect a fool. The sensitive person takes relationships seriously and tries to maintain them.

Verse 11 appears to relate to rebellion against the king's authority, and the "cruel messenger" to some dire calamity that will befall the one who rebels.

Verse 12 is a figurative way of describing the destructive consequences of folly. What could be angrier than a mother bear whose cubs have been taken from her?

In verse 13 the law of retribution is again stated. Do evil, and you bring evil upon yourself.

Verse 14 graphically warns against starting a quarrel or fight. These things begin with some minor unpleasantness, but, like a tiny hole in a dam through which the water only trickles at first, unless stopped the thing will break out into a disaster.

Verse 15 is a proverb taken from the law court. A crooked judge who declares the guilty to be innocent and the innocent to be guilty is a disgrace and an abomination to the Lord. Of course, the truth of the proverb is generally applicable. We all either uphold or disown righteous causes.

Verse 16 tells us what we ought already to know, namely, we cannot buy wisdom; it is not for sale. There are a lot of things that money won't buy.

Proverbs honors friendship as a great gift. Verse 17 is one of numerous teachings on this subject. See chapter 27. The constancy of friendship is celebrated here. "Friend" and "brother" are one and the same in this verse. A friend is a true brother.

For an interpretation of verse 18, see 6:1-5.

In verse 19 "makes his door high" refers to the building of one's house on a high place, the sign of pride and arrogance. Figuratively, if you elevate yourself above others, expect trouble from them.

Verse 20 is one of many statements in Proverbs that God will not permit the wicked to prosper in life. Life simply will not work if it is built upon crookedness and perversity.

Verse 21 is a common theme in Proverbs. See 10:1 and 17:25.

Verse 22 reminds us that illness is not simply a physical disorder. The mind's attitude has weighty influence upon the body's condition. Here is an ancient insight which modern medicine increasingly acknowledges.

See comment on verse 8 for the meaning of verse 23. "Bosom" refers to the secrecy of offering the bribe. The briber pulls the money out of his inside coat pocket.

Verse 24 contrasts the singlemindedness of wisdom with the unfocused wandering of the attention of the fool. Young people now refer to this as "getting your head together." Paul said, "One thing I do" (Phil. 3:13).

See 10:1 for interpretation of verse 25.

Verse 26 acknowledges that there are times when the righteous suffer because they are righteous. To impose a fine upon or administer a beating to another because he is righteous is a grievous sin.

Verses 27 and 28 salute the virtue of self-imposed restraint in speech. The wise honor reserve and reticence of speech. The good person does not tell everything he knows. He knows how to keep his mouth shut when it is appropriate to do so. See also 10:19; 11:12; and 13:3. Verse 28 makes the witty observation that even the fool may pass for being wise if he keeps his mouth shut. Once he opens his mouth it becomes evident that he has nothing to say.

Chapter 18:1-24

The text of verse 1 is difficult, resulting in different translations in the King James Version and Revised Standard Version. The sense of the proverb seems best expressed by the Revised Standard Version and means that once a man has excluded himself and become a rebel he finds fault

with everything and everybody. It is a kind of defense mechanism to justify one's outlawry.

Verses 2-3,6-8,13,20-21 are all about the importance of speech. The
preoccupation of the Proverbs with the power of words to do either good
or harm evidences the importance attached to speech. Verse 2 makes the
simple observation that a fool has no interest in learning anything, he
simply likes to hear himself talk. Verse 4 recognizes the importance of
what one says. "Deep waters" and "fountain of wisdom" both presup-
pose that the speaker is a wise person. Verse 6, on the other hand, states
in contrast the result of a fool's talk. The fool by his talk stirs up trouble
and invites a flogging. Verse 7 states essentially the same thing. A fool is
found out and ruined by his speech. His words become a snare in which
he catches himself. Verse 8 recognizes the deliciousness of gossip. As
destructive as it is, we still enjoy it like a tasty morsel. Verse 13 deplores
hasty speech, "popping off," before one knows what one is talking
about. Find out the facts before you pass judgment. Verse 20 suggests
that speech is not "just talk," but is like work well done. From well-
chosen, thoughtful words comes deep satisfaction. Verse 21 goes further,
holding that the tongue exercises the power of life and death. Think
about that when you are "just kidding around."

Verse 3 states the law of consequences in yet another way. Contempt
and disgrace are the pay-offs for a life of wickedness.

Verse 5 has to do with injustice in the law court. The dishonorable
judge acquits the guilty and deprives the innocent of justice.

Verse 9 shows the relationship between laziness and destructiveness.
This proverb reflects the high value placed upon work by the wise. Lazy
people are destroyers of the public good and of their own well-being.

Verse 10 lays claim on "the name of the Lord" as the refuge of the
righteous. In the Old Testament "name" stands for character, or the person referred to. "The name of the Lord" is who God is. In God's nature
and being there is refuge, a safe place, for the righteous.

Verse 11 states that wealth is a source of power, an observation that
we see illustrated in our time. No moral judgment is passed on that fact
of life in this proverb, but it should be remembered that in general the wise
considered wealth a sign of God's approval.

Verse 12 is about the sin of pride. Sometimes we have to suffer destruction before we are willing to be humble, and only in humility is there true
honor.

Verse 14 reminds us of 17:22. If your spirit (your inner being) is in good condition you can endure your body's sickness, but if your spirit is in poor condition everything is wrong. Sickness of the mind and spirit is much more harmful than sickness of the body.

Verse 15 is one among many in Proverbs saluting the virtue of intelligence and wisdom. Only the truly educated know how little they know, and are therefore open to learn wherever they can.

Verse 16 acknowledges the common fact that to give a gift opens doors otherwise closed. There is no moral judgment passed here, but it is easy to see how a gift may become a bribe.

Verse 17 relates to evidence in a trial. In an argument of any kind the first person who tells his story is very apt to make a strong case for himself, and it is only when the other side is heard that the truth emerges. This is a good proverb for people involved in marital conflict. "There are two sides to every question."

Verse 18 reflects the ancient practice of deciding between contenders by casting lots, or as we would say today, "drawing straws."

Verse 19 observes that one makes a strong ally of a brother by helping him, while quarreling erects barriers between the two. Notice that the King James Version translates the verse differently. In this case the King James Version is closer to the Hebrew text, the Revised Standard Version translating from the Septuagint, a second-century BC Greek translation.

Verse 22 celebrates a good marriage as one of the important blessings of life. A good wife is a favor from the Lord.

Verse 23 is an observation about the power of money. The poor have no money, but the rich can throw their weight around and run over others simply because they are rich.

Verse 24 again celebrates friendship (see 17:17). In this case it is noted that not all who claim to be friends are. If you have a real friend you are fortunate; he is like a brother.

Chapter 19:1-29

Verse 1 again preaches that it is better to be poor and honest than crooked and a fool. There is a subtle inconsistency in the logic of the wise about poverty. On the one hand it is taught that God blesses the righteous with wealth and good health, and on the other the poor, honest person is honored by the Proverbs.

Verse 2 stresses the importance of knowledge. If one runs off helter-skelter without adequate knowledge of his situation he invites his own ruin. Such a person may blame the Lord for his misfortune, but it is really his own folly that brought him to ruin (v. 3).

Verses 4 and 6 are companion statements acknowledging the common observation that wealth buys friends, if such hangers-on can indeed be called friends. Remember the prodigal son in the far country before his money ran out (Luke 15:13).

Verse 5 is an admonition against lying. Proverbs takes a position against bearing false witness.

Verse 7 deplores the common human frailty of deserting the person whose poverty makes him powerless and thus unable to help us. This verse is the only example in this major section (10:1 to 22:16) which is composed of three lines, rather than two or four.

Verse 8 observes that in the final analysis the one who acquires wisdom is helping himself. This may sound self-serving, but the fact is that we are responsible for ourselves more than we are for anyone else. One may want to know as much as possible in order to be a blessing to others, but in the process one helps oneself.

Verse 9 is a duplicate of verse 5, except for a minor difference in the second line.

Verse 10 holds up the incongruity of a fool being able to live in luxury or a slave to rule over noblemen. Both are outlandish situations, and scarcely to be conceived as possibilities.

Verse 11 honors the quality of being slow to lose one's temper, saying that the mark of maturity is the ability to overlook an offense. See 14:29 for another proverb making the same point.

Verse 12 acknowledges that the king is a powerful person whose attitude toward common people may either destroy or bring favor to them.

In verse 13 the burden of a foolish son is placed alongside the curse of a quarreling wife. The annoyance and debilitating effect of a continually dripping rain is picturesque.

The obverse side of the wife situation is given in verse 14. One may inherit wealth, but a man can account for the blessing of a good wife only as a gift from the Lord.

Verse 15 is another rebuke of laziness. This is a common theme in the Book of Proverbs. Sloth is like an anesthetic.

See 13:13 for an interpretation of 19:16.

Verse 17 suggests that kindness to the poor is more than an act of charity; it is a gift to the Lord, who will remember the kindness and repay. Jesus said as much: "as you did it for one of the least of these my brethren" (Matt. 25:40).

Verse 18 incorporates a basic principle in Hebrew thought: neglect of discipline in rearing your child is not an act of love but of lovelessness. Only through discipline can you guide him aright. Neglect his discipline and you may see him go astray and destroy himself. See 13:24; 23:13.

The meaning of verse 19 is uncertain because the Hebrew text is unclear. It appears to say that if you rescue a man who lets his temper get away with him you will have to do it again and again. He will not exercise self-control so long as you are available to bail him out.

Verse 20 points to the goal of life—wisdom—and proposes that it comes only through being communicated by the teacher or parent. Verse 21 emphasizes the sovereignty of God. Man may make all kinds of plans, but their fulfillment is contingent upon God. See James 4:13-15.

In verse 22 the emphasis is upon the importance of covenant loyalty, in Hebrew *hesedh*, often translated "kindness" or "mercy." See Micah 6:8. The two lines of this proverb are related by the contrast between loyalty to one's commitments and being an untrustworthy person. Poverty is nothing to aspire to, but poverty is a more desirable condition than being a liar about commitments.

Verse 23 has an unusual form in that it appears to be a triplet rather than a couplet. This proverb emphasizes one of the familiar themes of the book, namely that reverence for the Lord is the key to blessedness. The specific promise here is freedom from harm.

Verse 24 is a humorous reference to the behavior of the lazy person. He is so trifling that he will not even feed himself. Proverbs is a strong recommendation for industriousness and thrift. See also 6:6-11; 12:27; 20:4; 22:13; 24:30-34; 28:19; 30:10-31.

How do we learn? Verse 25 says that the simpleminded, the unlearned, may require the example of punishment. But the intelligent person does not require physical force in order to learn, only instruction. Tell him, and he will get the point.

Verse 26 expresses abhorrence of physical violence against parents. It reflects the Hebrew respect for age. Parent abuse is a disgusting crime, as is child abuse.

"Only" (v.27) is not in the Hebrew text, but is used by the translators to attempt to clarify the teaching that we are to be "doers of the word, and not hearers only" (Jas. 1:22).

Modern readers of the Proverbs will note that a lying witness is held in contempt. This is a book of old-fashioned morality, in which things are either right or wrong, black or white. The second line of this proverb is a vivid metaphor describing the hungry eagerness of the wicked to consume iniquity, like a thirsty man gulping down a drink of cold water.

Verse 29 is a synonymous proverb stating as an inevitability the punishment of those who make light of the Word of God.

Chapter 20:1-30

Another of the "old-fashioned" concerns of Proverbs is drunkenness. See 23:19-21,29-35;31:4-7. "Mocker" is the familiar word which is often translated "scoffer." Beverage alcohol may make a fool out of a person, as an estimated fifteen million alcoholics in the United States in the 1980s attests.

Noted in 16:12-15 is the high esteem in which a righteous king was held by the wise, and the scorn for a wicked king. See also 20:8, 26,28; 21:1; 31:1-9. Verse 2 warns against incurring the king's wrath. Be careful not to offend the king; it could be fatal.

Verse 3 cautions against getting involved in brawling. The fool goes about picking fights or responding to challenges to fight. The wise person simply avoids such lowbrow behavior.

Verse 4 is a down-to-earth saying about the necessity to do the work of preparation if you expect to reap the reward. Plowing was done in the fall after all the crops were harvested. But the lazy man is too trifling to plow. He supposes that the land will produce a crop without his labor. When harvesttime comes again he will have none.

Verse 5 recognizes that a person's inner thoughts may be as deep as a bottomless pool, so deep that the person may not himself be able to know them. But the wise person will be able to penetrate the deepest depths of personality. This is precisely the work of the modern counselor with his or her counselees.

There is a world of difference between the claim of righteousness and the performance of it. Many a person merely "talks a good game" of being upright (v. 6).

Verse 7 proclaims the great blessing of having a righteous father. That is the best inheritance one can have.

For interpretation of verse 8 see verse 2. "Winnows all evil" means he sifts out the bad from the good.

Verse 9 declares the universality of human sinfulness. See Romans 3:10-18.

On verse 10 see 11:1; 16:11; 20:23. A dishonest merchant who uses weights and measures which are false is a disgrace in God's eyes. Such a merchant defrauds the poor.

Verse 11 states that character is revealed by one's deeds, even if one is a child whose character is still being molded. What we are comes out in the way we behave.

Verse 12 is a saying which celebrates the Hebrew belief that God is the author of everything, including the parts of the human body. Therefore, nothing is unclean in itself, and all things belong to God who made everything. The stewardship of the body is taught here.

Verse 13 is another admonition about the hazard of being lazy. See 19:24 for interpretation. The practicality of this proverb reminds one of the familiar modern saying, "Early to bed and early to rise, Makes a man healthy, wealthy, and wise."

Verse 14 is a humorous reference to one of the oldest practices known in bargaining. The prospective customer disparages the article he has his eye on, shows great disinterest in it until he gets the price down, and then goes away with it bragging about his bargain.

Verse 15 celebrates the value of wisdom. "Gold" and "costly stones" are metaphors symbolizing the objects of highest worth.

Verse 16 is duplicated in 27:13. Both denounce the folly of going on the note or standing bond for a stranger. To do such a foolish thing will likely "cost you your shirt." "Foreigners" in the second line may be "foreign women," as the text is unclear, but the meaning is the same. See also 6:1-5.

The temporary enjoyment of evil is the subject of verse 17. "A mouth . . . full of gravel" would not be pleasant.

"Plan ahead" is the sense of verse 18. Nothing should be undertaken rashly, including war. Do not let emotion outweigh reason. See Luke 14:31 for Jesus' use of this metaphor.

Verse 19 admonishes against associating with gossips. If you do you may find that you are the subject of much loose talk, because a gossip loves nothing better than to broadcast others' secrets.

Verse 20 is still another observation concerning the duty to honor one's parents. "Lamp" in line 2 represents life.

Verse 21 declares that there are no shortcuts to long-lasting prosperity. This interpretation of the prosperity of the wicked was one way of explaining the absence of justice which permitted the wicked to prosper and the righteous to be poor. The argument is that the prosperity of the wicked is temporary. In the final analysis, wrong cannot win.

Was Paul thinking of Proverbs 20:22 when he wrote Romans 12:19?

For an interpretation of verse 23 see verse 10.

Verse 24 claims the sovereignty of God. God is the one who orders man's steps. Line 2 is a question which suggests that it is vain for us to try to understand all the mystery of our life. See 16:9 for a similar proverb.

Verse 25 deplores the practice of thoughtlessly taking religious vows, especially vows which involve the dedication of something one owns. Rash vows do not reflect much respect for God. Jesus denounced those who used religious vows ("Corban" meaning dedicated) as a way of avoiding giving deserved support to parents (Mark 7:11).

Verses 26 and 28 are additional words about the function of the king. See verse 2. In verse 26 the metaphor is of separating wheat from chaff by the ancient method of driving cartwheels over it. Verse 28 name three qualities that are becoming to kingship.

Verse 27 is a beautiful figure of speech recalling God's act of creating man different from all other animals, by breathing into him the breath of life. "Spirit" is the same word as *breath* in Hebrew. This inner "Godness," or conscience, is God's lamp, his searchlight, turned on man's inmost being.

Verse 29 does not represent the popular wisdom of today. Our age glorifies youth and despises old age. Youth culture, music, and styles in dress dominate American thought. See also 16:31.

Punishment, says verse 30, is good for us. It purges away evil. "Blueness" in the KJV refers to being beaten "black and blue."

Chapter 21:1-31

Verse 1 proposes that the king is an agent of the Lord, a stream of water, an irrigation ditch, which the Lord directs at will. See 20:2,8,26,28 for sayings about the king.

On verse 2 see verse 16: "Weighs the heart" is a common expression in Egyptian religious language, where the god of justice, Thoth, is depicted as weighing the heart of the deceased.

Verse 3 is close to the beliefs of the prophets. See Amos 5:22-24; Hosea 6:6; Micah 6:6-8. The meaning is plain: Sacrifice is a religious duty, but much more important are personal uprightness and justice with one's neighbors. The ethical demand of God is first.

In verse 4 "lamp" (RSV) is better than "plowing" (KJV) and is the translation achieved by a slight alteration of the Hebrew word used here. The sense of the proverb is that haughtiness and pride are central for the wicked, instead of humility.

Verse 5 commends diligence and condemns "get rich quick" schemes.

Verse 6 complements verse 5. Ill-gotten wealth attained by lying is a short-lived attainment.

Verse 7 declares that there is a law of retribution, and that it is inviolable. The wicked may not engage in violence without bringing destruction upon themselves. "Sweep away" is a figure of fish being caught and taken up in a net.

The Revised Standard Version translation of verse 8 makes the contrast between the wicked and the righteous more decisive.

Verse 9 is duplicated in 25:24, and the sense of it also appears in 21:19. The teaching is that any kind of privation is to be preferred over strife with one's spouse.

In verse 10 the observation is made that the perverse person has no regard for anyone, not even his neighbor. No one is safe at the hands of a wicked person.

For the interpretation of verse 11 see 19:25.

The Hebrew text of verse 12 is unclear. The sense of the proverb is that where the righteous sees the wicked go down to ruin.

Verse 13 says that we get in life what we give. Ignore the needs of others, and our needs will be ignored. None of us is invulnerable; we are only vulnerable at different places and times.

Verse 14 states a fact of life, without recommending it. The one who gives bribes gains influence or buys favors.

Was Paul thinking about verse 15 when he wrote in 1 Corinthians 13:6 that love "does not rejoice at wrong, but rejoices in the right?"

Verse 16 threatens death to the one who strays from the path of rectitude. "Rest in the assembly of the dead" means simply "die." This reference is to Sheol, the abode of the dead.

Verse 17 is an admonition against self-indulgence. Wine and oil were marks of affluence and ease. Wine was used at banquets, and oil was used to anoint the head with sweet-smelling fragrance. The "partying" man will never get rich by being a playboy.

Verse 18 expresses a thought strange to prophetic religion. In this verse it is suggested that, like wicked Haman, who in Queen Esther's day plotted the destruction of the Jews but was hanged on the gallows he had built for Mordecai, the wicked person will be punished instead of the righteous. The noblest concept of prophetic religion is that of the Suffering Servant (see Isa. 53), the righteous One who suffers in place of the wicked.

For an interpretation of verse 19 see verse 10.

The Hebrew text of verse 20 is difficult, but the Revised Standard Version translation seems to have captured the sense of the verse. It teaches that the wise man is conservative with what he has gathered, while the foolish man squanders whatever comes into his hands.

Verse 21 is a progressive statement in which the second line of the couplet is required to complete the thought of the first. It is a familiar sentiment, promising reward for the righteous.

Verse 22 celebrates the victorious power of wisdom. It is mightier than kinds of power ordinarily considered to be supreme. The figure of the walls of a strong city being scaled by the ingenuity of the wise is most expressive.

Verse 23 is a practical word of advice about not talking too much. If you keep your mouth shut, it will save you a lot of trouble.

Verse 24 is a definition of the "scoffer," one of the most obnoxious types of fool in the Proverbs. Pride and arrogance are his characteristic marks.

Verse 25 is another ironic statement about the lazy person. See 19:24; 20:4; 22:13 for other examples. The humor of the proverb is that the sluggard kills himself by starving because he is too lazy to support himself. He would rather go hungry than work.

The contrast between the wicked and righteous is in no place sharper than in their attitude toward money. "The wicked covets" it, but the righteous is openhanded in giving (v. 26).

Verse 27 has prophetic overtones (see also v. 3). God will not accept the sacrifice of the wicked, but to bring a sacrifice with evil intent and malice is a worse offense.

For an interpretation of verse 28 see 19:5; 20:9.

The image of the wicked in verse 29 is that of the person who has no shame. He has a brazen look. He does not avert his gaze, but stares others down. He knows no shame and is never embarrassed. The righteous, on the other hand, is considerate of others and concerned about the way they are affected by his behavior.

Verse 30 declares the absolute supremacy of God. No human ingenuity can overcome him.

Verse 31 is a natural follow-up of verse 30. There is perhaps no human effort which lends itself more to pride than does war. "The horse is made ready for the day of battle" refers to military preparedness. To bring the proverb's figure up to date to the twentieth century, the symbol would be about bombs and missiles. But in any time of history, it is God who gives victory. "Man proposes, God disposes."

Chapter 22:1-16

Verse 1 is an all-time favorite of parents who wish to instill in their children's minds the need for being well-thought-of. "A good name" is to be cherished as a precious possession.

Verse 2 is a declaration of the fundamental equality of all persons in God's sight. He made both rich and poor and regards them with equal concern.

Verse 3, repeated in 27:12, observed that the prudent (wise, reflective) man avoids trouble, while the simpleminded rush into it without caution, suffering as a result of their lack of judgment.

Verse 4 is an unabashed promise that the person who reverences the Lord in humility will be rewarded with the truly valuable benefits— riches, honor, and long life.

Verse 5 complements both verses 3 and 4. The contention is that life will not work for the perverse. The nature of the world which God has made makes it impossible to break the rules and get away with doing so. One can only break oneself on them.

Verse 6 summarizes much of the teaching of the wise. They held that nothing was more important than the rearing of a child in godliness. Discipline was an integral part of that training (see 13:24; 19:18; 23:13-14). No reward in life was more satisfying than to have a fine son (23:15-16), and no sorrow was greater than to have reared a foolish son (17:21). "Train up" means literally, to dedicate, as in the Temple. That idea has beautiful religious significance.

Verse 7 is a synonymous statement of a fact of life, namely, money talks. The rich controls the poor, and the lender is master of the borrower. Compare this verse with verse 2.

Verse 8 is about sowing and reaping. See Galatians 6:7-8.

"Bountiful eye" in verse 9 means literally "good of eye." Compare this statement with Matthew 6:22, which refers to a sound eye. See interpretation on 19:17.

Verse 10 is a synonymous proverb—the two lines saying virtually the same thing, which is that "scoffing" is the source of much evil.

Verse 11 in the Revised Standard Version expresses a logical thought extracted from an uncertain Hebrew text. The proverb is progressive, the two lines making a complete thought. The argument is that single-minded goodness and gracious speech will win the friendship of the king—a most desirable goal.

Verse 12 claims the omniscience of the Lord. See interpretation on 15:3.

Verse 13 is another humorous and sarcastic comment about the sluggard. See 19:24; 20:4; and especially 26:13, which is almost identical with 22:13.

Verse 14 is the only reference in Book II of Proverbs to the adulteress, whereas chapters 1—9 are extensively concerned with the problem. Compare this proverb with 30:20. Here the anger of the Lord is said to be visited upon the man who is trapped by the wiles of the adulterous woman.

In verse 15 there is another reference (see v. 6) to the discipline of youth. The sages believed that punishment was a necessary accompaniment of learning.

Verse 16 concludes Book II of Proverbs. This saying defends the rights of the poor against the unjust extortion visited upon them by the rich. In the light of the common identification of riches with the Lord's blessing, such words about the rights of the poor are a clue to the moral sensitivity of the sages.

Book III

22:17 to 24:34

Introduction and First Collection (22:17 to 23:14)

Look closely at these proverbs. Notice that they are four-line sayings rather than the two-line sayings of 10:1 to 22:16. This section of Proverbs is divided into an introduction (22:17-21); first collection (22:22 to 23:14); second collection (23:15 to 24:22); and third collection (24:23-24). Scholars note that much in this section is similar to an

Egyptian wisdom writing known as "The Instruction of Amen-em-ope," especially Proberbs 22:22 to 23:14.

Verses 17-19 introduce the sayings that follow, calling them "the words of the wise," and promising rich rewards if they are observed. "It will be pleasant" (v. 18) if you cherish them in your heart and have them together ready to come from your lips. The reason for making them known to the pupil is that he may put his trust in the Lord (v. 19). That is why the communication of these truths is imperative.

Verse 20 refers to the thirty sayings found between 22:22 and 24:22. Of these thirty, ten are similar to the "Sayings of Amen-em-ope," leading many scholars to the conclusion that there is some relationship between this section of Proverbs and the wisdom writing of Egypt. "Give a true answer to those who sent you" (v. 21), probably refers to the parents who sent the youth to the teacher's school. The teacher wants him to be able to show his parents how much he has learned.

Verses 22-23 comprise the first of the thirty sayings. This one has a prophetic overtone, for it champions the cause of the poor and afflicted, saying that the Lord will be their lawyer and their defender. It is noteworthy that Amen-em-ope has a parallel saying for verse 22, but none for verse 23. The belief that the Lord was defender of the poor is peculiarly Hebrew.

Verses 24-25 admonish the youth against close association with an angry man, literally "owner of anger," lest by such association the young man adopt his ways and become entrapped in anger.

Verses 26-27 are a warning against another type of folly commonly noted in Proverbs, that is, becoming surety for others' debts (see 6:1-5). The sense of verse 27 is "Unless you are prepared to pay, don't sign another's note, lest you lose your bed," a basic need, like your coat.

Verse 28, unlike most of the sayings in this section, is only two lines long. It recognizes the sacredness of boundaries. One of the ways a person's property could be stolen was to remove the landmark, but such landmarks were property demarcations which were maintained from generation to generation. See also 23:10. This saying may also refer to the need to keep property in the family, as indicated by the words, "which your fathers have set."

Verse 29 recommends skill (one form of wisdom) as a means of achieving recognition with the powers that be. The craftsman will always be respected as a master of his art, and will not be relegated to association with people who don't amount to anything. The literal meaning of "obscure" is "men in the dark."

Chapter 23:1-3 is a six-line poem concerning the mundane matter of table manners. Part of the teaching of the sage in the training of young men was to develop gentlemanly behavior, or manners. First, "observe carefully," see what is before you and who is at table. "Cut your throat rather than appear to be greedy," gobbling your food like a person of low breeding (v. 2, AT). This is a humorous saying. Finally, do not be deceived by the king's delicious food. There may be a price attached to his "wining and dining" you.

Verses 4-5 comprise the next saying. It is a warning against the deceitfulness of riches. Centuries later Jesus warned against the temporariness of wealth (Matt. 6:19-21). How many people have had this experience: their wealth "suddenly takes to itself wings, flying like an eagle toward heaven" (v. 5)!

Verses 6-8 admonish the youth about becoming enticed by a stingy man's offers of a banquet. He is "setting you up" for something. "His heart [that is, his thoughts, intentions] is not with you" (v. 7c). Verse 8 describes the unpleasant consequences of this deception. "Vomit up the morsels" may be literal food, or it may refer to the favors the rich but designing neighbor has given.

Verse 9 is a simple couplet which admonishes the youth not to waste his time talking to fools. A contemporary saying with the same meaning is about "a dollar chasing a nickel." See 26:4-5 for similar sayings.

For the interpretation of verse 10 see note on 22:28. The second part of this four-line poem (v. 11) calls the Lord "Redeemer," an honored role in Hebrew life. The redeemer, *goel* in Hebrew, was an avenger, a rescuer (see Job 19:25). See 22:22-23 for a parallel saying of the Lord coming to the defense of the poor.

Verse 12 is a synonymous couplet admonishing the youth to be a diligent learner. See 22:17 for a similar saying.

Verses 13-14 reflect the sages' belief that punishment is necessary to good teaching/learning. "Spare the rod and spoil the child" is an early American version of this thought. See 22:6 for further instruction on this subject.

Second Collection (23:15 to 24:22)

Verses 15-16 reflect the teacher's joy in the successful learning of his pupil. "Soul" in verse 16 ("reins," KJV) literally means "kidneys," believed by the Hebrews to be the seat of the emotions.

Verses 17-18 are an admonition not to allow the success of the wicked to create envy in the heart of the youth. Their success in life, while ignoring God, will surely be short-lived. There is a future (v. 18), and the righteous will not lose his reward. See Psalms 37, 73 for clear statements of this position.

Verses 19-21 admonish the youth against excess in eating and drinking. The drunkard and the glutton are persons who have devoted themselves to their appetites, and "their god is the belly" (Phil. 3:19). Poverty is the result of self-indulgence, in part because such excess brings on drowsiness (v. 21). A modern application of this truth is the scandal of the "three-martini lunch."

Verses 22-25 appeal to the youth to make his parents happy by being an earnest seeker after truth. "Buy" (v. 23) suggests that life is a series of transactions in which we exchange time, energy, and devotion for certain goods which we consider valuable. The highest good is wisdom, and the chief part of wisdom is reverence for the Lord.

In verses 26-28 there is a stern warning against being entangled by the wiles of a prostitute. Sexual immorality was denounced as a self-destructive sin. See chapters 5, 7, and 9 for extensive treatment of this subject.

Verses 29-35 are one of the sharpest, clearest arguments against alcohol abuse that one could imagine. Verse 29 asks six questions, each of which indicates the dire effects on those who get hooked by alcohol. Effects of alcohol are graphically described in the rhetorical questions: woe, sorrow, strife, needless hurts, bloodshot eyes. Who can expect such experiences? The person who engages in long-term, hard drinking. The picture conveyed by "tarry" is of one who sits down and keeps drinking until he finally drinks himself into drunkenness. "Mixed" in 23:30b is a reference to lacing the wine with spices to make it taste more exotic, and perhaps to make it more potent. Verse 31 has been translated, "Do not gloat over the redness of wine" (AB). The thought is that the alcoholic becomes entranced by the sparkle of the wine, its color, etc. He looks at it with the fascination of one who is captivated. It has taken away his self-control; he personifies it as though it was in itself something deserving his adoration. He is hooked on alcohol. One has become an alcoholic when one is no longer able not to drink.

Verses 32-35 describe the sad results of the life of alcoholism. It tastes so delightful, and is so much "fun" going down, but the results are tragic (v. 32). Alcohol distorts vision and muddles speech. One sees what is not really there, or fails to see what is, and one says things which would shame one if one were sober (v. 33). Verse 34 describes the reeling, out-of-control condition of the drunk. The "ground won't sit still" when he tries to walk, but is like the heaving of the sea, like trying to cling to the mast of a ship at sea. The drunkard gets beaten up, but he is so drunk that he does not even feel the blows—that is, he knows nothing about it until he wakes up and finds himself in a miserable state. Does that keep him sober? Not on your life. The first thing his body demands when he "comes to" is a drink of alcohol (v. 35c). Whoever has dealt much with alcoholism will appreciate the accuracy of this description of the alcoholic's behavior.

Verses 1-2 of chapter 24 warn against evil company. The way of the wicked looks inviting, but it is ruinous. See 1:10-19 for a full discussion of this admonition.

Verses 3-4 speak of life as the building and furnishing of a house. Wisdom and understanding are the most profitable associates in such an enterprise. See Matthew 7:24-27 for Jesus' use of the metaphor of house building.

Verses 5-6 argue that wisdom is mightier than physical strength. If you have to choose between brains and brawn, take brains. The illustration used is waging a war. Strategy is a more effective weapon than the force of numbers (v. 6). The history of Israelite victories in the early days confirmed this belief.

Verse 7 is a couplet, rare in this section, which says simply that the foolish man does not understand wisdom. It is too "high" for him; it is beyond him. So in the gate of the city where men meet to discuss important issues he has nothing to say.

Verses 8-9 denounces the "mischief-maker" (v. 8), who always has an "angle," who is forever scheming how to outwit and outmaneuver others to his advantage and their disadvantage. His cynicism (scoffing) is an abomination, a shameful thing, to all people.

Verse 10 is a two-line observation about faintheartedness. The Hebrew contains a play on words that cannot be expressed in translation. *Carah* ("adversity") and *car* ("small") catch one's attention. Life's pressures will show the kind of strength you have.

Verses 11-12 are a strong statement of social responsibility for those who are oppressed. The picture is of the downtrodden who have no one to defend them and are defenseless in their own power. We see them "stumbling" like poor beasts being driven to slaughter. A modern image of this scene is the Jewish victims of Hitler's gas chambers. Is there no one to rescue them? "Oh," says the self-declared innocent bystander, "I did not know this was happening" (v. 12). "Not good enough," replies the teacher, "for God tests our hearts. He knows whether you knew, and he will requite you according to the way you responded to what you knew" (v. 12b, AT). Jesus' parable of the last judgment (Matt. 25:31-46) should be read in connection with this warning in Proverbs.

Verses 13-14 say that what honey is to the mouth wisdom is to the mind. It is the superlative food of the spirit.

Verses 15-16 warn against plotting against the righteous, for although one might knock the righteous man down seven times, he can not be knocked out, but will come back, because the Lord is on his side. "Seven" is a favorite number in Hebrew thought, and signifies the ultimate or most. Such promises must have been most encouraging to righteous victims of exploitation and oppression.

Verses 17-18 begin with a noble sentiment, but end with an unbecoming sentiment. "Do not rejoice when your enemy falls" (v. 17) sounds like Jesus' Sermon on the Mount (Matt. 5:43-48). But the sentiment of verse 18 would not measure up to Jesus' standards. This verse warns that if you rejoice over the hard times your enemy is having, the Lord may turn his anger away from your enemy, and presumably turn it upon you. See 17:5; 24:29; 25:21-22 for other proverbs on this subject.

Verses 19-20 complement the two preceding verses. The sense of the statement is that it is idle to be envious of the success of evil persons. The reason is that there is no future in doing evil. Evil itself has no future. The "lamp [life] of the wicked will be put out" (v. 20). Sin does not pay. Compare Psalms 37; 73.

Verses 21-22 give additional support to the previously noted argument (see 16:12-15) that the king is in league with God and an emissary of the divine. Paul in Romans 13:1-9 takes this position about the authority of government.

Third Collection (24:23-34)

Verse 23a introduces what appears to be a brief appendix (24:23-34) to this entire collection which began at 22:17. "These also are sayings of the wise" clearly is meant as a statement introducing certain proverbs which are to follow.

Verses 23b and 24-26 speak out against showing favoritism in the law courts. For the judge to declare the wicked who are really guilty to be innocent is an abhorrence everywhere ("by nations," v. 24b). In short, even among pagans there is a sense of the outrage of a crooked judge who frees the guilty rather than rebuking them. As partiality in rendering judgment is condemned, fairness is commended (v. 25). Verse 26 has an interesting colloquial saying about "kisses the lips," apparently referring to the act of bestowing honor upon a friend. The honest judge who gives "a right answer" is like one who is a true friend.

Verse 27 carries the simple moral of the need to do things in proper sequence. Here the reference is to the time to get married. One should not marry first, then set one's affairs in order. That is the wrong order. First be able to support a family, then "build your house," a figure used to describe starting a family.

Verse 28 contains another admonition against bearing false witness, this time against one's neighbor. "Witness without cause" is to perjure oneself, a serious crime in any society where truth and justice are highly regarded.

Verse 29 is one of the several verses in Proverbs which express an ethic that is not merely pragmatic, but altruistic. This is against "paying back," doing to others as they have done to you. See Proverbs 20:22; 25:21-22 for similar examples of this noble thought.

Verses 30-34 are further statements about the despicable behavior of the sluggard (see 6:6-11; 19:24; 20:4; 22:13). Laziness is a vice condemned by the sages. The evidence of the evil of laziness is the neglected fields of such a man. The conclusion is that just taking it easy ("A little sleep," v. 33) will cause poverty and want to steal upon you unexpectedly.

Book IV

A Second Collection of Solomon's Proverbs 25—29

Chapter 25:1-28

Proverbs 25:1 provides the title to the next group of proverbs, comprising chapters 25—29, declaring that these proverbs come from Solomon and that they were "copied" by the "men of Hezekiah." King Hezekiah

was a contemporary of the prophet Isaiah in the late eighth century BC.
It was the time of the destruction of the Northern Kingdom of Israel, and
the flight of Samaria's religious men (including sages) to Jerusalem. Very
likely their coming stimulated fresh religious and intellectual activity,
and it may be that this collection of proverbs is in part, at least, one result of that increased activity. The five chapters of this section divide into
two parts. Chapters 25—27 are focused more on secular matters, such as
good manners and correct behavior, while chapters 28—29 are much
more religious in subject matter.

Verses 2-7 are on kingship. It has previously been noted that there is
an extensive treatment of the monarchy in Proverbs, most of the sayings
being favorable to the king. See 16:10, and numerous others. Verse 2
says that it is God's nature to be inscrutable, but kings have a special gift
for understanding mysteries. Verse 3 takes for granted that the king has
superior wisdom. Verses 4-5 compare refining silver with removing from
the king's presence any wicked persons. Silver is ready for the silversmith
after the dross has been burned out, and the king can do his work best
only when evil has been removed from his presence. Verses 6-7 admonish humility in the presence of the king or other great persons. Jesus used
this very example in Luke 14:8-11.

Verses 8-10 admonish against rushing into litigation against one's
neighbor. The passage begins with verse 7c, and makes the sensible
statement that it is better to try to settle a disagreement with a neighbor
privately, for if you go to court you may discover that what you thought
you saw really did not happen, and then you will be embarrassed and
gain a bad reputation.

Verses 11-15 relate to the importance of using the power of words
appropriately. Words are bearers of messages. A "word fitly spoken" is a
beautiful ornament. "Apples" (v. 11) is inserted in the English translations without any corresponding word in the Hebrew. The sense of the
passage is that fit words are a lovely ornamentation. Similarly (v. 12),
one who is able to listen to the words of a wise reprover has received a
beautiful present. Trustworthiness in giving messages (teaching?) is as
refreshing as cold snow during the autumn heat of harvesting the crops.
Verse 14 expresses the opposite thought. A man who goes about making
rash promises which he never makes good on is like the promise of rain
in clouds and wind without any rain falling. Finally, verse 15 extols the
virtue of gentle speech. Remember, "A soft answer turns away wrath"
(15:1). "A soft tongue will break a bone" is surely a picturesque way to

exalt the power of speech. There is power, not weakness, in calm and gentle words.

Verse 16 recommends moderation and self-control. Don't overdo anything. Too much of a good thing is a bad thing. See also v. 27.

Verse 17 is practical advice about how to get along with your neighbors. Don't make a pest of yourself. Many a potentially good relationship is ruined by too much closeness. "Familiarity breeds contempt." Robert Frost probably had this in mind when he wrote, "Good fences make good neighbors" (from "Mending Wall").

The destructiveness of a lying neighbor is described in verse 18. Such a person can do great harm. See the interpretation of verses 8-10.

Verse 19 warns against trusting a man who is inconsistent and undependable. The proverb means you cannot depend upon a bad tooth that may break off, or upon a foot that may give way. No more can you depend upon an unreliable man.

One who "sings songs to a heavy heart" (v. 20a) is insensitive to the other's condition. Happy songs and heavy sadness are contradictory, just as are cold weather and coatlessness, or putting "vinegar on a wound." (This would make it sting.) Whereas songs are appropriate in many circumstances, they are ill-timed if the other person is full of grief.

Verses 21-22 contain another statement about how to respond to an enemy. It begins with a noble challenge, but ends on a sour note of pragmatism. "The Lord will reward you" (v. 22b) is a crass appeal to buy the Lord's favor by kindness toward an enemy. Paul quotes this proverb in Romans 12:20, with the exception of the final line.

Verse 23 uses a nature metaphor to teach that certain behavior inevitably produces certain consequences. Does the north wind drive "away rain" (KJV) or bring "forth rain" (RSV)? These opposite interpretations of the text reflect a difference in the function of the north wind. But the point is unchanged by either translation. Cause produces consequence. Backbiting always produces anger in those who are its victims.

Verse 24 is a duplicate of 21:9. See it for interpretation.

Verse 25 is a proverb of comparison—"Like this, like that." Is there a more vivid metaphor than "cold water to a thirsty soul?" So welcome is good news.

Verse 26 is another proverb of comparison, this one lamenting the spoiling of a good man by the pollution of the wicked. To see a good man corrupted by an evil person is a sad loss, like having a pure stream polluted.

Verse 27 has a plain meaning despite the wide difference in the translation of line 2 between the King James Version and the Revised Standard Version. The first line says simply "a little honey is about all the palate can stand" (see 25:16). The second line as rendered in the Revised Standard Version, which does not follow the Hebrew text very closely, means, "so be sparing of compliments; don't overdo it" (AT).

Verse 28 says plainly that whoever loses self-control leaves himself defenseless, as a city whose walls have been broken down. Self-control is an important virtue, as the wise understand life.

Chapter 26:1-28

Verses 1-12 of this chapter deal with the behavior of a most despicable kind of fool, *kesil*, who is swinish, thick-headed, and brutish. The point of verse 1 is that neither snow in summer nor rain in harvest are conceivable in Palestine. As absurd is the thought of giving honor to a *kesil*, "a fool."

Verse 2 does not specifically mention the fool, but it is clearly related to unwarranted and idle behavior such as would be characteristic of the fool. This is a proverb of comparison, the likeness being drawn from the aimless winging of a sparrow or swallow. A curse spoken without cause is just as aimless.

Verse 3 suggests that a fool cannot be controlled by reason, any more than a horse or an ass can be so guided. Stronger methods are required. The whip, bridle, and rod are all for the same purpose.

Verses 4-5 are antithetic to each other, the first saying that the wise person will not engage a fool in serious conversation lest the wise descend to the fool's level. The second says the opposite, namely, that the wise should not ignore the folly of the fool, lest he suppose that the fool's folly is really wisdom, his arguments unanswerable.

Depending upon a fool to deliver a message, says verse 6, is like cutting off your own feet (in today's vernacular, "Like shooting yourself in the foot") or inviting violence upon your cause.

Verse 7 is a proverb of comparison, a simile which compares a fool to the uselessness of a lame man's legs.

Verse 8 is another proverb of comparison, this one containing a somewhat obscure reference to "one who binds the stone in the sling." The sense of the proverb seems to be that as absurd as fastening a stone so tight in a sling that it could not be thrown is the giving of any kind of distinction to a fool.

Verse 9 compares the uselessness of a stick from a thornbush in the hand of a drunkard with the speaking of wisdom by a fool. Actually, more harm than good can come from such a situation.

Verse 10 in both King James Version and Revised Standard Version is largely reconstructed, neither being able to decipher the meaning of the obscure wording of the Hebrew. The Revised Standard Version reading states that to hire a passing fool is no more reasonable than an archer who scatters arrows at random.

Verse 11 is a statement of inevitability. The dog comes back to his vomit, and the fool is a repeater of folly. (See 2 Pet. 2:22.)

Verse 12 says that a self-conceited man is worse than a fool, and that is a very bad thing to be.

Verses 13-16 are further condemnations of the sluggard. Verse 13 is virtually a repeat of 22:13. Verse 14 alludes to the lazy man's habit of turning over in bed and going back to sleep. Verse 15 is very similar to 19:24, making humorous reference to the sluggard as one so trifling that he won't even feed himself. Verse 16 is another proverb of sarcasm about the sluggard. He thinks he is smarter than seven wise men.

Verse 17 says that one who meddles in others' quarrels is as foolish as one who foolishly grabs a strange dog by the ears, risking getting bitten by the dog.

Verses 18-19 deplore unbridled practical joking. The man who continually plays deceptive games at his neighbor's expense, thinking them hilariously funny, is like a crazy person who goes about recklessly throwing firebrands, or shooting arrows, or spreading some form of death. Such practices are highly explosive.

The practical nature of chapters 25—26 is nowhere better illustrated than in verses 20-21. Here the sense of the sayings is that it takes provocation to start a quarrel or a fight. The provocation may be an idle rumor (v. 20), or a person spoiling for a fight (v. 21), but somebody starts it, like throwing wood on a fire.

For an explanation of verse 22 see 18:8, which is a duplicate.

The sense of the proverb (v. 23) is plain. An earthen vessel is a cheap, ordinary pot. Putting a glaze on it may make it look fine, but it is worth little. So are smooth, slick lips (talking) with an evil mind ("heart").

Verses 24-26 denounces the sugary-talking person whose words beguile you to your face, but who inwardly despises the very people he courts with his flowery flattery. Hatred in the heart may be concealed beneath dissembling with the lips (v. 24). Do not trust such a person, for his heart contains seven (an ultimate number) abominations, and despite his guile, he will be exposed and denounced in the public meeting of the congregation.

Verse 27 teaches the inevitability of retribution. "Pit" means setting a trap. He who seeks to ensnare others traps himself. We get what we give, harming ourselves with the very harm we sought to perpetrate.

Verse 28 is simply a further elaboration of the truth stated in verses 24-26.

Chapter 27:1-27

Verse 1 admonishes the youth who learns it not to suppose that anyone can absolutely guarantee the future. Just when you think that you have it made, life pulls the rug out from under you. See James 4:13-16 on this thought.

Verse 2 recommends appropriate modesty. Don't blow your own horn. Give other people an opportunity to discover your good qualities by themselves, then they will praise you.

Verse 3 says poetically that it is hard to put up with the burden of a fool's provoking behavior which is heavier than stone or sand. See the interpretation of 26:1-12.

Verse 4 deplores the destructiveness of jealousy. Wrath and anger are synonymous expressions. Such violent outbreaks may do extensive damage, but they are temporary and pass, while jealousy is a seething, consuming emotion which burns on and on relentlessly. Anger is bad, but jealousy is worse because it is more destructive.

Verses 5-6 commend openness in relationships. It may not seem like love if someone who really cares for you rebukes you, but rebuke is a truer love than passive endurance of inappropriate behavior. Many a parent puts up with a child's bad manners, supposing that to correct the child would be unloving, when lack of correction indicates indifference to the kind of person the child is becoming. The "wounds of a friend" (v. 6) are truer than the "kisses of an enemy." Not everybody who flatters you to your face is to be trusted.

Verse 7 teaches the simple lesson that people who have too much are soon bored with even the finest ("loathes honey"), but if one is truly hungry (physically or spiritually) one will be eager to be fed whatever is available. To such a person "bitter is sweet."

Verse 8 deplores the wandering man who puts down no home stakes. He is like a bird lost out of the nest.

Verse 9 is difficult because of the uncertainty of its second line. The King James Version rendering of the line is closer to the Hebrew text than is the Revised Standard Version, which has translated the second-century BC Greek Septuagint text of the verse. A contemporary translation renders the verse more clearly: "As perfume and incense gratify the senses/ So a friend's cordiality strengthens one's spirit" (AB).

The general sense of verse 10 is that one should stick to and rely upon family and close friends. The verse is a triplet, line 1 warning against forsaking those close to you. Line 2 warns against burdening your brother with your troubles, lest you alienate him (compare 17:17). Line 3 avows that one is better off to have a close neighbor than even a brother if the brother is distant, either geographically or emotionally.

Verse 11 is an admonition and a plea to the youthful student to make his teacher proud of him by his wisdom, lest the teacher be reproached for having done a poor job of teaching. The true test of the teacher's ability is the student he produces.

Verse 12 is a duplicate of 22:3. For interpretation see it.

Verse 13 is a duplicate of 20:16. See its interpretation.

The meaning of verse 14 is similar to verse 6, namely, be wary of effusive praise from another, for he may be cursing you under his breath. The picture here is of one who works at praising others. Rising early in the morning, he overdoes it and incurs suspicion.

Verse 15 reflects the sages' view of marriage. Nothing is better than a good one, and nothing worse than a bad one. See 19:13b; 21:9; and 25:24 for similar statements.

Verse 16 is a continuation of the argument in verse 15. The text of this verse is impossible to translate in its present condition. The Revised Standard Version rendering is an effort to make it clear by translating it to say that an argumentative wife cannot be controlled any better than wind can be captured or oil grasped and held onto.

Verse 17 reflects the importance of good associations. "Iron sharpens iron" refers to the use of a file to sharpen a metal blade. So other people influence and affect us. Therefore, it is crucial that the people you associate with be a good influence on you.

Verse 18 makes the point that "the labourer is worthy of his hire" (Luke 10:7, KJV). This verse encourages the servant to be faithful in serving his master, promising that such loyalty will be rewarded.

Verse 19 is a beautiful picture of the inevitability of one's inner character being reflected in one's outward behavior. Like water mirrors your face, your actions will not belie who you are.

Man's insatiable craving is the subject of verse 20. He can never get enough, no matter how much of life he has experienced, but always cries, "More!" So it is with the abode of the dead (Sheol) and the deepest pit of death (Abaddon). People keep falling into the pit of death, but it is never filled.

The first line of verse 21 is identical with 17:3a. See above. The second line completes the thought here by saying that a man's true test comes in the manner in which he responds to praise.

As men grind wheat into flour by crushing it between a pestle and a stone jar (mortar), so you would have to press the folly out of a fool. It is so much a part of him that only with great difficulty can folly be extracted from the fool (v. 22).

Verses 23-27 give practical advice about the solid values of the life of the farmer/shepherd. One may not grow rich as a herdsman, but riches and kingly power do not last forever (v. 24). But when winter comes, the lambs provide clothing for the shepherd, and the goats provide milk for all his family. Such solid benefits are to be considered seriously instead of the flashy gains of commerce and the royal court. Don't feel sorry for the farmer; he is not as poor as you imagine.

Chapter 28:1-28

Verse 1 observes the value of a clear conscience. If you know inside that you are guilty, you will see a threat in every casual remark or glance.

Verse 2 states that when a nation falls into sin its government becomes unstable. But good rulers tend to produce stability in the nation. The last few decades of Israel's life illustrated this proverb, as the nation was subjected to repeated overthrow of its king.

Verse 3 deplores the disgusting sight of a poor man oppressing another poor man. Such a condition is like a driving rain that destroys the crops. What would be ordinarily thought of as helpful turns out to be destructive. Such is the oppression of the poor by the poor.

For exposition of verse 4 see 13:13. The "law" here is the law of Moses.

Verse 5 is antithetic, contrasting evil men's blindness to the meaning of the law with the righteous ones' clear knowledge. Those who do not understand do not wish to know. "Completely" is a statement of hyperbole.

Verse 6 is a familiar saying in Proverbs. See 15:16; 16:8; 19:1.

Verse 7 distinguishes between the wise son who honors his father by following the instruction of his teacher with the foolish son who disgraces his father by associating with gluttons.

Interest was not allowed by the law of Moses. Here the threat is made that those who do this to the poor will have it taken away from them by God who will give the ill-gotten gain to the poor (v. 8).

Verse 9 states that prayer offered by a man who despises the law of God is an abomination. Such prayer has to be hypocritical.

Verse 10 is a three-line proverb affirming the law of retribution.

Verse 11 says that there is no fool like a rich fool. He sees himself as a self-made man, but the righteous poor man will see through his facade and know him for what he is.

Verse 12 says that there is great rejoicing when righteousness is victorious, but when wickedness wins, get out of the way.

There is a familiar prophetic note expressed in verse 13—God requires contrition, not sacrifice. One must not only confess but forsake sin to obtain God's mercy.

Verse 14 declares blessed the man who unqualifiedly reverences the Lord, and contrasts him with the man who hardens his heart.

Verses 15 and 16 include another denunciation of a wicked king. See 16:10.

Verse 17 is difficult, but the clearest meaning is reflected in the Revised Standard Version. A murderer should not be assisted in his effort to flee.

For a proverb similar to verse 18 see 10:9. The promise is for deliverance to the righteous and disaster to the wicked.

Verse 19 is one of many recommendations of industriousness as opposed to laziness. The work ethic is important in Proverbs.

Verse 20 implies that get-rich-quick schemes are nearly always questionable. Better to work steadily, accumulating slowly.

Verse 21 is against bribery, suggesting that a poor man may be tempted to perjure himself for a piece of bread.

Verse 22 deplores the greed which devours a man who becomes obsessed with money. What a common sight he is in all times!

The evil of flattery is exposed in verse 23. See 27:5-6 for a similar saying. Rebuke, if true, is better than flattery.

Verse 24 denounces the person who is cruel to his parents, who manages to escape responsibility for their care, who "robs" them by claiming that what they are due is sacred. See Matthew 15:4-6.

Verse 25 contrasts the fate of the man who is "proud" (KJV) or "greedy" (RSV)—"has a wide appetite" (Hebrew)—with the one who puts his trust in the Lord.

Verse 26 has the same message as the one preceding it. To trust in one's own ingenuity is foolhardy.

Whoever disregards the needs of the poor, averting his eyes, will be cursed. On the other hand, the generous will prosper (v. 27).

Verse 28 is a variation of verse 12, reversing the lines.

Chapter 29:1-27

Verse 1 observes that a stubborn man refuses to learn anything and is finally brought low.

For interpretation of verse 2 see 28:12,28.

Verse 3 is a version of the many observations in Proverbs about the dangers and folly of licentiousness. See Proverbs 2, 5, 7, 9.

Verse 4 is one of many comments on the blessing of a good king and the curse of a wicked one. See 16:10.

Verse 5 says flattery is a trap set by the flatterer.

Verse 6 contends that evil is its own undoing, like a snare, while the righteous man has no such threat to his well-being.

Verse 7 states that the poor have rights—an important moral affirmation—which are recognized by the righteous but unknown by the wicked. What does the wicked care for the rights of the poor?

Scoffers by their cynical attitudes and behavior inflame a city and arouse it to violence, according to verse 8.

For interpretation of verse 9 see interpretation of 26:4-5.

The second line of verse 10 has to be emended, either to say that the just will seek to protect the blameless, or that the wicked will seek to destroy him. The proverb points out that the wicked will always find the righteous a threat.

Verse 11 observes that the fool does not control his temper, but he who does keep his temper under control is wise.

Verse 12 is one of many proverbs about the power of the king to do great good or wreak havoc.

Verse 13 is quite close to 22:2. See its interpretation.

Verse 14 celebrates the presence of a just king who does not discriminate against the poor. The social justice concerns of the sages are freely expressed in the Proverbs.

See interpretation of 22:6 for the meaning of verse 15.

The wicked may be on top for a while, and when they are life will be hard for the righteous, but they cannot ultimately prevail. Sooner or later, evil will fail (v. 16).

Verse 17 is a familiar recommendation of discipline for children.

Verse 18 is one of the most familiar in Proverbs, especially in the King James Version. The statement, however, is not about the importance of vision, but concerns the crucial role of the prophet. Where prophecy disappears there is no self-control among the people. The moral power of the prophetic word is celebrated.

Verse 19 recommends physical punishment for slaves, on the ground that the slave will not learn from merely being told. Verse 21 should follow verse 19, as it is a logical progression from it. Do not pamper your servant, lest he claim a son's position.

Verse 20 deplores talking without first thinking things through.

Verse 22 denounces the man of unbridled temper. See interpretation of 15:18.

Verse 23 is an antithetic proverb on the results of pride versus humility. Notice the play on words between "low" and "lowly."

Verse 24 denounces the partner in crime who goes to court, takes an oath under a curse for lying, then declines to tell what he knows about the crime in question.

Verse 25 refers to fear of what other people may think or say.

In verse 26 the customary high opinion of rulers is reversed to say that men ought to trust in the Lord rather than in kings.

Verse 27 recognizes that the wicked and the righteous look at life from opposite poles, and each is an offense (abomination) to the other.

Appendixes
30:1 to 31:31

First Appendix: Dialogue Between a Skeptic and Believer (30:1-9)

Verse 1 gives the title of this brief collection. "Agur" and "Jakeh of Massa" are not Hebrew, but Arabic words, suggesting that the origin of this collection is non-Hebraic. See Genesis 25:14 and 1 Chronicles 1:30 for references to "Massa." Verses 1-9 constitute a dialogue between a skeptic and a believer. Verses 2-4 state the position of the agnostic, who does not believe that we can know anything about God. Verses 5-6 are the believer's response, saying that God is trustworthy and has revealed himself through his Word. Verses 7-9 are a prayer of the righteous that God will grant him knowledge of the truth and his daily bread.

Is verse 2 a sarcastic way of saying, "I am not wise like some men claim to be?" Or is it a straightforward expression of humility? The text does not make it clear, but it is plain that the speaker is skeptical about the possibility of knowing God.

"Knowledge of the Holy One" (v. 3) refers to religious knowledge.

Verse 4, a series of rhetorical questions, is very similar to some of the questions of the Lord to Job in Job 38. See Ps. 139:7-12.

Verses 5-6 give the believer's answer. The word of God will stand the test of examination; it is true. God is a refuge for those who trust him. Do not try to put words into his mouth or deny what he has said, lest you be rebuked and proven a liar.

Verses 7-9 are a closing petition asking for two things: To be trustworthy, not to engage in falsehood; and secondly, to be neither rich nor poor. Too much tends to cause one to become proud and to deny the Lord. Too little, and one may resort to stealing.

Second Appendix: Admonitions and Proverbs (30:10-33)

Verses 10-33 are a series of admonitions and proverbs. Verse 10 is an admonition to refrain from talebearing to a master about his servant. Mind your own business and you will stay out of trouble.

Verses 11-14 list four types of evil men. Each verse begins with the word "generation," (KJV) or "there are those" (RSV), meaning a class of people. These four evil types are: despisers of parents; self-righteous; arrogant and proud (lofty eyes); and devourers of the poor.

There follows now (verses 15-33) a series of numerical sayings. The first is about four insatiable things: Sheol (death); the woman without children (barren womb, which was a disgrace to a woman); the thirsty earth parched for water in a dry land; and fire which devours (vv. 15-16).

Verse 17 is an exception among the numerical proverbs of this section. It admonishes and rebukes the youth who is inclined to make fun of or ignore the rights of his parents, inexcusable behavior for a Hebrew youth.

Verses 18-19 contain four wonders: how a great bird is able to fly through the air; how a snake moves without legs and feet; how a ship plies the waves; and the wonder of lovemaking.

Verse 20 is another isolated verse, this one describing the callous behavior of the adulteress. "Wipes her mouth" shows her unconcern about her behavior. She says of adultery, "No big deal!"

Four unbearable types of persons are described in verses 21-23: a slave who gets to the throne; a fool with a full belly; a woman who marries after she had given up hope of a husband; and a maid who supplants her mistress in her husband's affections.

Four small but wise things are the subject of verses 24-28: ants, because of their industriousness (see 6:6-8); badgers, who are ingenious about building their houses; locusts, who have order without a king; and the lizard, who can climb up any wall, even the king's palace.

Verses 29-31 describe four stately things: the lion; a strutting cock (or a war-horse—the text is obscure here); a he-goat; and a king strutting before his people. There is an implication here that the king may be something of a show-off.

Verses 32-33 admonish self-restraint. If you have been "blowing your horn" too much, or planning evil against someone else, put your hand on your mouth (i.e., stop it). If you push too hard you will get bad results, as when milk goes sour, or a nose bleeds from too much pressure upon it.

Third Appendix: A Queen Mother's Counsel (31:1-9)

Verses 1-9 are addressed to an unknown king, Lemuel of Massa (see 30:1) and are admonitions from his mother about lust and strong drink (vv. 2-7), and an exhortation to rule justly (vv. 8-9).

"Son of my vows" (v. 2) refers to the vow a mother might take in order to have God's aid in getting a son (see 1 Sam. 1:11). The word "son" in each case here is Aramaic, not Hebrew.

Verse 3 admonishes against becoming involved with wicked women who will destroy a king's powers. Verses 4-5 warn the young king about the dangers of strong drink. Such deadening of the senses should be reserved for those who are in great pain and are dying (vv. 6-7).

"Open your mouth" (vv. 8-9) means to speak up for the rights of the poor and oppressed. The king's obligation to defend the defenseless is a very high ethical standard. (Noblesse oblige, nobility obligates.)

Fourth Appendix: The Good Wife (31:10-31)

This is one of the best-loved passages in the Bible. It is a beautiful description of a wife who complements her husband. She is many things to him. Inasmuch as Proverbs says so much against the wicked woman who is unfaithful to her husband or seeks to entice the young man, this poem is all the more important. The poem is an acrostic, each succeeding verse beginning with a succeeding letter of the Hebrew alphabet, making the poem easier to memorize.

Verse 10 affirms her great value to her husband.

Verse 11 says that her husband is confident that she will not squander his money and plunge him into bankruptcy. Verse 12 completes the thought of her competency.

Verse 13 describes her industriousness in making clothing.

Verse 14 tells of her shrewdness in marketing, not merely buying what is most convenient.

Verse 15 reports her energetic, work-oriented daily schedule.

Verse 16 suggests that her husband even trusts her to make major decisions such as buying property and planting a vineyard, a most unexpected quality in an Old Testament wife.

Verse 17 describes a woman who is not afraid of hard work. She gathers up her skirt and rolls up her sleeves to go to the field.

Verse 18 salutes the fact that she burns the midnight oil in her labors.

Verse 19 relates to her weaving skills, although the Hebrew word translated "distaff" is a word whose meaning is unknown.

Verse 20 extols her generosity to the poor.

She is not fearful of winter, for her family is dressed warmly (v. 21). She provides herself with a luxurious wardrobe, as she is a woman of distinction (v. 22). This is attested also by the fact that her husband is honored at the gates (i.e., he is recognized as a leader, v. 23).

Verse 24 is an additional reference to the good wife's industriousness and enterprising work. She trades with the merchants, selling her wares.

Verse 25 says that she is a woman of dignity and honor, and is unafraid of the future because she is confident and secure.

Her attainments are also in the realm of the intellectual (v. 26).

Verse 27 once more celebrates her industriousness.

Verse 28 proclaims her children's and husband's appreciation of her. They call her "blessed," and praise her as above all others.

Verse 30 disparages charm and beauty, for they are superficial and temporary. Reverence of the Lord is the crucial virtue.

Verse 31 says that she deserves the rewards her own labor produces, and that she will be honored in the public meetings. No wonder this poem is loved wherever the Bible is read.

ECCLESIASTES

Introduction

One of the surprises of the Bible is that Proverbs and Ecclesiastes stand back to back in the Old Testament canon. If one believes that the order of the list was itself divinely ordained, it makes for some interesting speculations. The reason is that these two books present their messages from opposite points of view concerning the nature of God, man, and nature.

Proverbs is a collection of mainly two-and-four-line maxims based upon the conviction that God has ordained an orderly, predictable, and discoverable system by which the world operates. Proverbs is in the mainstream of Old Testament thought. Although it is Wisdom writing, which means that it comes at truth from the position of observation rather than from the prophetic stance of revelation, it stands with the Prophets and the Law as far as its teachings are concerned. Simply put, those teachings are that God has created the world, is directly related to it, has ordained a system in which there are invariable consequences to man's obedience or disobedience, and that God has made all this available to man through revelation and nature.

There are notable differences between Proverbs and the writings of the prophets. One important difference has to do with focus. The prophets are concerned with Israel, Yahweh's special people who are bound in a covenant relationship with him. The covenant requires obedience for God's special blessing, and warns that disobedience will bring punishment. The Book of Proverbs is no less committed to God than are the prophets, but its emphasis is upon individual people rather than the people of Israel, and its understanding of the law of reward and retribution is not based upon the covenant but upon God's universal law. To Proverbs, right is right, wrong is wrong, and there is no ambiguity about such matters. Nor is there any great mystery about them, for a person can know what God requires. He learns it through observation and by paying attention to his "fathers," either his parents or his teachers. The

92

Book of Proverbs is classic Wisdom writing because it announces its conclusions as universal laws of life learned through observation, not through revelation.

Ecclesiastes is also Wisdom writing. But there the similarity between Proverbs and Ecclesiastes ends. Whereas Proverbs announces with confidence that life operates in orderly, predictable fashion, Ecclesiastes denies that man can gain access to the way the universe is structured or that man can predict anything save his own death. Life is perplexing, nature contradictory, and existence wearying. God is "up there" somewhere, but he is remote and has chosen to relate to people only from a distance, if at all. Ultimate values are few and far between. The best one can do is to live one's life day by day, enjoying the simple pleasures, and trying not to claim greater knowledge of God than is available.

Based upon its teachings one asks, "How did this book get into the Bible?" That question has been asked many times. The fact is that whether to admit it into Scripture was hotly debated by the two major schools of Jewish thought in the first century before Christ. The school of Hillel, considered to be the more liberal school of Jewish thought, admired the rationalistic spirit and honest candor of Ecclesiastes, and wanted it included. The school of Shammai believed Ecclesiastes was not devout enough and wished it excluded. When the canon of Hebrew Scripture was fixed at the Synod of Jamnia about AD 100, Ecclesiastes was included. Its inclusion was based mainly upon the fact that the name of Solomon, as suggested in 1:1, had become attached to the writing.

Whatever human factors were involved in its inclusion, we can rejoice that in God's providence Ecclesiastes is a part of our Bible, for it contains some of the most important teachings of Scripture. Ecclesiastes provides a balance to those who think and talk glibly about God. It brings up short those who are inclined toward presumptuousness in their claims to know the divine will. It is a sobering book. It teaches reverence for God, although it claims no personal relationship with him. Perhaps most important of all, this book compels the reader to take a serious look at the way he is living his life, the priorities he has established, and the things of God which he is inclined to take for granted. Even beyond these positive teachings, the absence of a sense of God's personal presence and the sense of sadness that pervades Ecclesiastes cause the Christian to affirm more strongly his faith that "God was in Christ, reconciling the world" (2 Cor. 5:19, KJV).

The Nature and Origin of Ecclesiastes

The philosophical nature of this book is evident in its search for a rational understanding of existence and a basis for ethical living. As has already been noted, the author rejected as unprovable the data of revelation. His basic thesis is "Vanity of vanities! All is vanity" (1:2). From the statement of this severe judgment about life, he proceeds with the recitation of experiences which in his view support the conclusion he has announced.

One can better understand Ecclesiastes by putting it in perspective of other Old Testament Wisdom writings. As previously noted, Proverbs is a collection of assured conclusions. There is no hint of philosophical or speculative wonder about life's meaning. This is the way it works: Do this and you get that; do the other and you get the other back. Job, also a Wisdom writing, raises some questions about this unequivocal position of reward-retribution. Does it always turn out that the righteous are blessed and the wicked punished? Are there no exceptions? Job himself is such an exception. The Book of Job turns upon the issue of a righteous man for whom the "system" does not work. The man is not simply unusually righteous in God's eyes; he is "blameless" (Job 1:8; 2:3). There is none like him on earth. He is classic man, man as God intended Adam to be. Yet this blameless and upright man suffered catastrophe after catastrophe. The coming of three friends to console him turned out to be the occasion for the examination of the issue of reward and retribution. The friends were confident that Job's grief was just and evenhanded punishment for his sins, and they admonished him to repent so that God could restore him. He on his part was unable to confess any wrongdoing and was driven by their insistence to the place of accusing God of unfairness. The entire issue was then subsumed by God's personal appearance "out of the whirlwind" (38:1). The theophany makes the issue of reward-retribution secondary, almost irrelevant. God never told Job that he did or did not deserve what he suffered. He came to him with the message that he, God, is God. And that experience was enough to bring Job to repentance and peace with God.

Notice, now, how Ecclesiastes goes beyond the position of Job. Neither Job nor Ecclesiastes is satisfied with the doctrine of reward-retribution. Neither believes that life is a system which man can observe and always be assured of being healthy, wealthy, and wise. But Job came out where the prophets were—in an encounter with God. God put in an appearance. God dealt with Job personally. God spoke to him, rebuked him, and comforted him. This personal encounter is the climax of the Book of Job. It is what makes it such a towering confession of faith.

But there is none of that in Ecclesiastes. The author's God is real but remote. He is not only personally unknowable, his ways are inscrutable. If there is a moral order, it is hidden from our eyes. In Ecclesiastes the reverent questioning of Job has become denial. The position of Job that there are exceptions to the rule of strict reward-retribution has been abandoned in Ecclesiastes, its position being that if there is a moral order, a "way the system works," it is hidden from man's eyes and may not be discovered by his reason. Further, we may not expect to have God show up and explain himself to us.

In the thought of these three Wisdom writings, there is a movement from the unquestioning certainty of Proverbs, to the exception to the rule insisted upon by Job and the appearance of God, making the issue of reward-retribution of less importance to Job, to the outright skepticism concerning our knowledge of God proposed by Ecclesiastes.

Historical Influences

Are there any historical factors which might account for this movement from the thought of Proverbs to that of Ecclesiastes? Probably. The origins of Proverbs may be as early as Solomon. The book represents a somewhat self-assured, sanguine feeling about God's relationship with Israel. Its concern is about morals and manners. There is a right way and a wrong way to do everything. For generations and centuries, the prophets had been telling the history of God's people in terms of their obedience or disobedience. When Israel suffered defeat at the hands of her enemies, or when famine overtook the Land, it was because God's people had been disobedient. When they repented, God would restore his blessings. The cycle of blessing—disobedience—punishment—repentance—blessing was seen as the clue to understanding Israel's history.

The Exile struck a terrible blow to that confident reading of God's relation to Judah and Jerusalem. Much of this faith position was invested in the continuation of the Davidic monarchy and the preservation of Jerusalem and the Temple as the visible "place" of Yahweh. With the Babylonian Exile both king and Temple were no more, and Jerusalem herself lay in ruins. One of the theological repercussions of this disaster was the reforming of the doctrine of identification of the cause of Yahweh with a Davidic king. After the Exile, there was no king. Jewish scholars did not abandon the doctrine of a Davidic monarch to perpetuity, but they redirected it to begin looking for an ideal King, a "type of David," a Messianic figure who would be David's descendant.

Another result of the Exile's shattering effect was that some Jewish thinkers began to restate the entire reward-retribution position. Perhaps there was no such exact, tit-for-tat, relationship between act and consequence, after all. "Speak tenderly to Jerusalem, . . ." wrote one of the greatest of all the prophetic voices, "[for] she has received from the Lord's hand double for all her sins" (Isa. 40:2). Here was no *quid pro quo* arrangement. Something awesome had taken place in the Exile. Judah had been twice punished. Had she been punished both for her own sins and for the sins of others as well? Had she suffered vicariously? Is there a "Suffering Servant"? This thought claimed the mind and heart of some great Hebrew prophet who wrote the last part of Isaiah after the Exile had happened.

Another who felt that the reward-retribution doctrine no longer described God's relationship with his people was the author of Job. A third was "Qoheleth," the writer of Ecclesiastes. Both Job and Ecclesiastes are probably post-Exilic writings. Ecclesiastes is noted by scholars to be written much in the style and grammar of late Judaism, dating perhaps from the fourth century BC. The book contains many Aramaic expressions and uses two Persian words—the Persians being the liberators of the Jews in captivity toward the end of the sixth century BC. Both thought and language suggest a late dating for Ecclesiastes.

The name of the book is something of a misnomer. It was derived from the designation of the author in 1:1 as "Qoheleth," a word coming from the Hebrew word, *qahal*, meaning "assembly, gathering, congregation." Qoheleth is the "assembler," the one who calls the congregation together. Therefore, by extension, he might be called the preacher or the teacher. The name "Ecclesiastes" in the Latin and English Bibles comes from the Greek word for assembly, or congregation, *ekklesia*. If *ekklesia* is the Greek equivalent of the Hebrew *qahal*, then *Ecclesiastes* would be the Greek equivalent for *Qoheleth*. This, then, is the Book of "The Teacher," or "The Preacher." He is the leader or speaker in the assembly.

Life as Mystery (1:1-18)

The thesis of Qoheleth is set forth unmistakably in the opening words which follow the superscription: "Vanity of vanities! All is vanity." The word *vanity* in Hebrew literally means breath or vapor and indicates the transitoriness, instability, and emptiness of life. All of the things people count upon to give permanence and substance to human existence are no more than a vapor rising in the morning air and disappearing before the sun.

Verses 3-11 cite evidence for the validity of the thesis that life is aimless. "Gain" (v. 3a) in Hebrew is *yithron*, and means what is left over from a transaction, the profit from a sale, and thus the net which one realizes from some effort. Qoheleth argues that the net gain of all man's toil is zero. Let him run ever so fast, work ever so hard, strive with all his might—it matters not. Man is essentially on a treadmill.

Four pieces of evidence are now submitted to defend the thesis of the vanity of all human effort. The first is that generations rise and pass away with monotonous regularity. "Sunrise, sunset," goes a ballad. Qoheleth sees nothing changing at all. Life is circular, not linear. The human race is going nowhere; it is simply repeating the tiresome routine of life and death. All that is constant is the stage, which is the earth. There is a new cast in every generation (v. 4). The other three witnesses to the weary repetitiousness of life are the movement of the sun, the blowing of the wind, and the flow of the seas (vv. 5-7). Qoheleth lived in a cosmological world in which it was supposed that the sun rotated around the earth. The earth was believed to be flat, the "under" side of it being the place of darkness where the sun hastens (literally "pants") to get back to the place of rising. The sun's routine is not haphazard; it is totally programmed to eliminate any change. On the other hand, the wind is designed for haphazardness and randomness. You never can tell where the wind may blow. It has its circuits, too, just as the sun does, but they are not as definable as are the sun's. The sun is routine, the wind is random, and the sea is an endless frustration. The streams keep on running into the sea, but the sea never gets filled up. In short, the world system is a kind of Rube Goldberg invention: Wheels turn, belts turn other wheels, things move, but nothing is happening. There is much movement, but no progress.

Humankind and the natural order both display an appalling lack of meaningful progression. Wherever Qoheleth looks or listens (v. 8), he can find no satisfaction. There are no words to describe his dismay at life's lack of purposefulness (v. 8a). "Weariness" is the most apt expression of what he feels. Verses 9-11 deny that there is anything new under the sun. Past and future have everything in common, for the future is only the past done over. Life is like a B-grade movie, run again and again on the screen. The only thing that changes in the program is the audience. The people seeing the movie suppose that they are seeing something new, but they are not. It is the same reel rewound. The reason people suppose the movie is new is that they have no communication with their predecessors. The disjuncture between one generation and the next is the reason why each generation thinks that its experiences are unique (v. 11). As it has been with those who went before, so it is with us, and so it will be with our successors.

For explanation of "the Preacher" see the introduction (v. 12). From this verse it is implied that Solomon is the author, but this is almost certainly not the case. The writer is using Solomon as the classic representation of wisdom. Not only is Solomon used as the example of one who was wiser than all others, but he is appealed to because a king is supposed to have power to do what he wants to do. The point is that the wisdom and power of even a Solomon would not be enough to alter the way things are. The futility of wisdom and effort is seen in three frustrations. One is in man's inability to find happiness (v. 13). Qoheleth thinks that only the stupid and unknowing could possibly be happy. The more one knows the less one can be joyous. God has given man an impossible assignment. He has given mankind only enough wisdom to know that he is unable to solve life's riddles, so that he has doomed mankind to frustration.

The second frustration is man's inability to set the world aright. The king has seen it all; he has surveyed the entire spectrum of human endeavor, and it is a "striving after" (literally, "feeding upon") wind (v. 14). Why does he feel so futile? Because, "What is crooked cannot be made straight and what is lacking [missing, left out] cannot be numbered (v. 15). Life, in other words, is fixed and inexorable. What is, is. No amount of struggling and striving will change anything. Man is not in a dynamic partnership with an active, involved God. God has completed the order and set people in it to do the best they can. The wise person learns how the order works and submits to it. Verse 15 is in the form of a proverb, suggesting that it is to be taken as a conclusion about life, a summing up of a good chunk of experience.

Not only is life without the possibility of improvement, being fixed and immutable, but it is also shadowed by impenetrable mystery. The king next declares himself to be a singular person so far as wisdom and knowledge are concerned (v. 16). Nobody outdistanced Solomon in being wise. "Solomon's wisdom surpassed the wisdom of all the people of the east, and all the wisdom of Egypt" (1 Kings 4:30). With such authority, he makes the sober announcement that he has concluded that there is nothing to be gained in either wisdom or folly. He had not simply concentrated on the better half of the spectrum of human thought—wisdom. He had also "applied my mind" to know "madness and folly" (v. 17). He knew the sensible side of life, and he knew the crazy side as well. And there was not "a dime's worth" of difference between them. For one who represents the cause of wisdom, such pessimistic conclusions are sobering.

Verse 18 appears to be another maxim (as v. 15), a summing up and conclusion of the argument presented. Moffatt translates verse 18: "The more you know, the more you suffer:/the more you understand, the more you ache." That is gloomy indeed.

The Futility of Customary Values (2:1-26)

If chapter 1 states the general thesis of Qoheleth that the world may not be understood nor its ways deciphered by man, chapter 2 examines the traditional and customary values of people, showing the futility of each as a way to make life worthwhile. There are four pursuits named here, and it will be noted that there is a certain progression in their ordering. These are almost like Shakespeare's seven stages of man. When you see these four put together you will be almost compelled to say, "Yes, that is the way most of us go about doing our lives."

"Let me experiment with pleasure and have a good time!" Qoheleth said to himself (v. 1, AB). Perhaps Qoheleth should be credited for chasing pleasure with deliberate intention, going after it with his eyes open. Most of us run after it simply because its allure is irresistible. He deliberately set out to determine if pleasure could bring him the sense of meaning which his mind and heart craved. Further, here is one who as king has the power to claim whatever he desired. Most of us are not that unlimited in what we could afford or get away with. He could do whatever he wanted, have whatever he desired. The end of that experiment? "But behold, this also was vanity" (v. 1b). The laughter of pleasureseekers was empty, its sounds echoing through the hollow chambers of his soul, and of the fruits of pleasure he could only say, "What use is it?" (v. 2). Qoheleth says that he really went about this search for meaning through self-indulgence in a serious way. He investigated the merits of wine to stimulate the body and pamper it without losing control. He gave serious thought to the subject of being a sensible drinker. All the time he kept his mind in control of his body (v. 3). He had no intention of becoming a drunk, or of debasing himself by losing control of his appetites. At the same time, he enjoyed dallying with folly (v. 3b). After all, a man has got to have a little foolishness along the way, or life gets unbearably dull!

So he lived on the street called "Folly," his idea being to use it as a temporary address. But he never intended to settle there permanently, and he did not want to be too closely identified with the people who lived on Folly Street. It was something of a holding operation for Qoheleth. It was an interim activity. He would give himself unreservedly to pleasure, make a thorough examination of that subject, while he was trying to determine what are man's true goals (v. 3b). Man has only a "few days" to live in this world. His is a limited engagement. How best use the time? Well, while he was working on the answer to that most important question he would see if pleasure, unrestrained and uninhibited, might be a clue. It was not. When he had exhausted all its invitations to self-indulgence he had to admit, "This is not the answer. This is vanity."

Next, Qoheleth turned his attention to building an empire for himself. He would become a person of enormous wealth, with all the trappings of the wealthy and successful. "I made great works" (v. 4). How do the rich show that they are rich? "I built houses and planted vineyards for myself; I made myself gardens and parks, . . . I made myself pools from which to water the forest of growing trees" (vv. 4b-6). Notice in the text how many references the writer makes to "myself" and "I." He was consumed by self-serving work. Whatever he did, the object of his affection was Number One—Qoheleth. No doubt the neighbors of Qoheleth were impressed by the sight of his expansive holdings in real estate and the development of his grounds with gardens, vineyards, and orchards. When he gave a party, people must have come and whistled softly to themselves at the sight of such opulence, with male and female slaves, male and female singers, and many concubines fluttering around the big man of the town, Mr. Qoheleth.

Or was it now Judge Qoheleth, or Senator Qoheleth? "So I became great and surpassed all who were before me in Jerusalem" (v. 9). People tipped their hats when his carriage passed them on the street. They sought his favors, and vied for the privilege of saying that they were on a first-name basis with him. He was an important personage. But he could only ask himself, "Is this all?" See verse 11 for his judgment on the worth of wealth and power.

He had sought the obvious pleasures of the body and found them lacking in the power to satisfy the heart. He had turned to wealth, empire building, and power. But these, too, left only emptiness in his soul. One thing that human ambition strives for remained—wisdom. He would become a philosopher! All other achievements are as nothing by comparison. He sees himself as "the king" (v. 12b). The king is the ultimate, the last word. The king holds all the records—the record for the most pleasure, the greatest wealth, and the largest accumulation of power. Who can outdo the king? Nobody. What is the successor of the king to do to distinguish himself? He is bound to be in the king's shadow. He can only repeat, and hope to approach, the king's records. One thing remained, wisdom. Ah, not everybody is wise. There are those who exhaust the possibilities of self-indulgent pleasure, and those who become rich and powerful, but how many are wise? Wisdom is man's highest good, Qoheleth surmised (v. 13). It is the difference between light and darkness. Qoheleth turned therefore to the pursuit of wisdom to give meaning to life.

Soon he wearied of the effort, for he had to admit to himself that when he dared lift his eyes and look into the future neither wisdom nor folly looked that much different from one another. The further you got from them in your perspective the more futile they both appeared (vv. 15-17). The same end awaits both the wise and the fool. One fate comes to all (v. 14). "Why strain your brain trying to be wise and understand?" (v. 15, AT). Both die, and are soon forgotten (v. 16). How many years or decades will it take before all our names are nothing more than entries in the records of vital statistics?

Such melancholy thoughts left Qoheleth close to despair. Why knock himself out? Everything he gave himself to evaporated like morning mist in the air. To try to take hold of something substantial and permanent was like trying to catch a handful of fog. Do you aspire to build a great estate in order to pass it on to your son? Qoheleth asks himself, "If I do, how can I be sure that he will not be a fool?" (v. 19, AT). Yet he will have mastery over what I worked so hard to gather. How many generations is it from poverty to riches to poverty again? Three?

Contemplating the futility of life when taken at long-range, Qoheleth turned his mind (heart) over to despair. The man who has toiled with "wisdom and knowledge and skill" (v. 21) must leave it to lazy, shiftless heirs who will only squander what the collector got together. "What has a man from all the toil and strain?" (v. 22). It seems hardly worth the struggle. There is so much pain, vexation, and stress connected with living out one's days. Why, even at night the mind does not rest (v. 23b), suggesting the worrier who gets up in the morning as tired as when he went to bed.

Verse 24 brings Qoheleth to the first statement of his conclusion about life. Where is meaning to be found, if not in pleasure, wealth, power, and wisdom? It is to be found in the enjoyment of the everyday pleasures of life—food, drink, work (v. 24). Subsequently Qoheleth adds to those three common pleasures a fourth—love of one's spouse (9:9). These common ventures are a gift from God, but about them there is a certain predetermined character. It is not as though you could decide to have all these simple joys, and then just begin to enjoy them. Even the little pleasures of life are from the hand of God (vv. 24b-25). And how does God decide to parcel these out? Verse 26 may be interpreted to say that God rewards those who are righteous while punishing the sinner by setting him to the task of gathering for the enjoyment of the one who has pleased God. Such an interpretation would support the religious pragmatism of Proverbs, but does not sound like Ecclesiastes. Qoheleth has already said that one of the reasons for despair is the realization that the good and wise person may gather a large heap of this world's goods only to have it squandered by a fool. Could he then in the very next verses suggest that those who get wealth are the ones who deserve it? That seems unlikely. What does seem consistent with Qoheleth's thought is that there is a great mystery about why some have wealth and power and others do not. He can only conclude that it is because that is the way God orders things. God seems to like some people better than others. Jesus would not have agreed. But to Qoheleth this demonstrates the vanity of trying to be successful in worldly terms.

Everything Happens According to God's Schedule (3:1-15)

One thing seems certain to Qoheleth—life is predetermined and ordered by God. That is why he wrote in the verses at the end of chapter 2 that God gives to those who please him. Here in verses 1-8 there is a clear statement of the inevitability of life. "Season" in verse 1 comes from a verb which means "to be fixed." God has prearranged the events of life. "For every matter under heaven" (v. 1b), there is a proper occasion. Everything happens when it must happen. Man's freedom? He has none, except to decide how he will react to the inevitabilities.

Note that the theme of the famous poem of verses 2-8 is the cyclical nature of existence. In endless repetition, life swings backward and forward between the poles of opposites, like a pendulum of a self-winding clock. The theme is the proper time. There is an appointed time for everything. Man can go with it or be crushed by it. He cannot alter it. "A time" does not refer to "appropriate" or "timely," but to necessity. Qoheleth is not saying, "Pick the right time for the right behavior. One doesn't laugh at the widow's weeping over her husband's coffin." That may be true, but it was not Qoheleth's meaning. He is saying that whatever happens to us happens because that is the way God arranged it.

The list of activities Qoheleth mentions are representative of the ordinary ventures of human existence. Life oscillates between life's commonalities. "To cast away stones" (v. 5), according to a Jewish Midrashic commentary, was a euphemism referring to marital sex, and to "gather stones" was to refrain from the act. In each of the examples of everyday activities, the point is that our lives are lived in the going back and forth between opposites, and that God has prearranged all of this so that man's freedom is an illusion, except for his choice of how he will respond to life's prearranged appointments.

The doctrine of Qoheleth comes perilously close to fatalism. He recognizes that himself, and it is one of the reasons why he must find a reason for man's life which comes out of his response to the events which God has prearranged. "What gain has the worker from his toil?" (v. 9) is simply a restatement of the conclusion of chapter 2. However, now he elaborates that general conclusion with five others—verses 10-15.

The first (v. 10) suggests that perhaps the meaning of life is that God knew that man needed to be busy and has therefore given him plenty to do. There is work to be done, even if all man's labor is insufficient to alter the cosmic scheme of things.

Verse 11 is one of the most provocative in the entire Book of Ecclesiastes. The first half of the verse is plain. "Beautiful" has the meaning here of "appropriate," or "fitting." God had no accidents and made no errors in his creative work. As Genesis 1 says, God saw that his creation was "good," that is, beautiful. The second part of this verse is troubling. What is meant by "eternity"? Was Qoheleth gazing into the future and wondering if there is an eternity in the sense in which we Christians understand the term? Inasmuch as this book was written probably as late as the fourth or third century BC, that is at least possible. Qoheleth may be saying that God has created in man the unquenchable fire of longing for eternal life, yet has hidden from man's eyes the game plan which God is using to bring this about. Man, the aspirer, is forever frustrated in his reach for the stars. He believes that the "intimations of immortality" are no illusions, but he must live without absolute knowledge. Perhaps that is the role of faith. Remember, however, that Qoheleth knew nothing of the resurrection of Christ. We must not read into his words a meaning which is not there. What we can say with assurance is that Qoheleth saw the created order as just that, an order, "beautiful," and made by God, but he also felt that man must accept his limitations and not be frustrated because he cannot grasp everything that God has done.

Verses 12-13 are the third conclusion drawn from the observation that there is a fixed time and season for everything. This conclusion restates the principle already enunciated, except that the principle here is expanded to say that enjoyment is itself a gift from God and is approved by God.

Verse 14 reiterates the doctrine of the fixity of all things by the decree and hand of God. What God makes lasts. Man cannot undo it, alter it, or delay it. Nor can he advance it. God has made reality as it is, so that man will have proper awe and fear of him.

Verse 15 adds one idea to the statement of fixity in the preceding verse. Not only are things fixed; they are also recurrent. Whatever is happening now has happened before, and whatever happens next year, or next century, has already happened. Life moves in cyclical form. "God seeks what has been driven away" (v. 15b) is best understood as referring to those events which have passed across the stage of human history. They are not gone—"driven away"—forever. God will bring them back across the stage in his own good time.

How Can Mortal Man Understand the Injustice of the World?
(3:16 to 4:3)

In this passage Qoheleth reflects sadly upon two observations about life—the injustice of the world and the oppression of the powerless. He cannot understand why a just God would allow it to happen. Although he has already taken the position that life is an unfathomable mystery to man's mind, he still wonders why injustice and oppression are permitted. What is God up to? Why does he do nothing about it? There is no satisfactory answer.

Then he suggests two tentative answers. The first is that God will surely tend to it in his own good time (v. 17). Do you see the prosperity of the wicked? Do not fret about it. God will take care of the wicked when he is ready to do something about it. The second tentative answer is that injustice and oppression are permitted by God so that God can teach man a much-needed lesson, that since he is of the earth, he is earthy. He may have eternity in his mind, but he is still a "beast," and shares the fate of the beasts (vv. 18-19). They are made of the same materials, and both are perishable. What advantage has man over the beast? None, for all came from the dust and return to it (v. 20). Verse 21 requires some attention. The prevailing view among the Hebrews was that at death all meaningful life ended. Sheol, the abode of the dead, was a great shadowy place beneath the earth where the souls of the dead were kept in limbo. Nearly every other ancient people of the Near East, including the Egyptians, Babylonians, Canaanites, and Greeks, had some form of belief in the afterlife. Usually these beliefs were associated with the fertility of nature and its annual rebirth. The Hebrews found such beliefs especially obnoxious because they usually resulted in some rite of worship in which fertility was exalted and nature worshiped. The Hebrews believed that Yahweh was the maker of nature, and he only was to be worshiped. Verse 21 suggests that Qoheleth is aware that there are those who argue (as the Persians did) that at death the soul of the deceased rises to be with its Maker. Qoheleth is unwilling to embrace this doctrine, although he surely must have known that if it were true it would make a cosmic difference between man and beast. Because he cannot believe that it is true, he concludes that there is no such great difference. Both are destined to the dust.

Verse 22 repeats the conclusion that, things being what they are, a person should adopt a view of his personal existence which allows him to enjoy fully the small pleasures and satisfactions of his earthly existence. There is no mountaintop upon which he can stand, as Moses stood on Mount Nebo, to gaze across and see with his own eyes the Promised Land that lies beyond his earthly existence.

Not only is the future hidden from the eyes of man, but the present also leaves him baffled. Why so much oppression in the land? Does God not behold the tears of the oppressed? Qoheleth sees them and is distressed. Is God not distressed? Who are the oppressors? They are the ones with the power, and that is why they oppress. Who are the oppressed? They are the powerless, with none to defend them. And who gives out power? God. (See 4:1.) Contemplation of this depressing reality leads Qoheleth to make the extreme statement that it is better to be dead than alive, and better yet never to have been born, for once you are born there is no way to escape being involved in this sorry scheme of things (4:2-3). However, one needs to contrast the pessimism of this statement in 4:3 with that of 9:4, where Qoheleth expresses a different view about the value of life.

The Folly of Competitiveness (4:4-12)

In this section, using a number of proverbs, Qoheleth warns against the folly of striving to get ahead of one's neighbor. Verse 4 serves as the key to the passage. All toil and skill in work are the result of trying to out-do your neighbor. "Competition is the soul of trade" is one of our own capitalistic maxims. Qoheleth rejects competition as a worthy motive for getting ahead. It is vanity.

Then follow, back to back, two proverbs (vv. 5-6). The first denounces laziness, the folding of the hands. Such indolence results in a condition in which the fool "eats his own flesh," that is, he devours his capital. He isn't producing anything; he is only consuming. That is obvious stupidity, besides being laziness. On the other hand, much is to be said for a life of quiet reflection (v. 6) rather than of obsessive, stress-filled effort to get ahead of one's competitor. Qoheleth's view of the good life will not find many sympathetic adherents among those who are committed to being "Number One."

Verses 7-8 expand further on the folly of killing yourself to get ahead. Qoheleth sees a person without heirs who toils ceaselessly, his eyes never satisfied with the wealth he has already accumulated. It is self-evident that he works not out of a sense of need but out of greed. "How much is enough?" asks a prominent minister. The answer is nearly always, "Just a little more than I now have." Paul was on target when he wrote, "For the love of money is the root of all evils" (1 Tim. 6:10). As Qoheleth has observed, the man who is consumed with greedy desire for gain never stops to ask himself, "For whom am I toiling and depriving myself?"

The advantages of cooperation over cutthroat competitiveness are noted in verses 9-12. "Two are better than one" (v. 9a) is the theme of this brief statement. They hold one another up, whereas one who is alone has only himself to support him in time of danger. They keep one another warm in cold weather, and they form a mutual protection society against attack. Qoheleth would have many questions about our vaunted rugged individualism.

The Folly of Fame (4:13-16)

Some folks want to be rich. Others want to be famous and powerful. Both are consuming and self-defeating desires, in Qoheleth's view. A poor and wise youth is more admirable than an old and foolish king (v. 13a). This was probably a well-known proverb. Qoheleth uses and expands upon it. The "old and foolish king" may well once have been young and poor himself; he may even have once been in prison, but rose to be king. As we might say today, "He has forgotten where he came from." So he no longer listens to anyone. He refuses to take advice or heed warnings that as he rose from obscurity to the throne there may be some young person out there just waiting to unseat him. Was the writer remembering Saul and David?

Another aspect of fame is its temporary nature. See the king with all the people admiring and saluting him? He will soon pass from the scene and those who come after him will not remember him with the acclaim accorded by his own generation (v. 16). Fame, like riches, is a poor reliance. Qoheleth pronounces "Vanity of vanities" upon it.

Take Worship Seriously (5:1-7)

The dimensions of Qoheleth's thought are already clear to us. He is committed to a life of contentment with the simple, everyday pleasures of life—food, drink, work, family. He believes that excessive ambition for money, power, or fame is folly. Having made that position clear, the remainder of the writing is an elaboration of these principles in a series of applications and admonitions. As a teacher, Qoheleth is committed to giving good advice to those whose care is his responsibility. So it is that he speaks a word of advice about propriety in worship.

The first thing to be careful about when you go to worship is your attitude. "Guard your steps" (v. 1). Don't saunter in, saunter through, and saunter out of church. You have come into the presence of the awesome God. Would you so casually pay a visit to the President of the United States, or would you try to look and act your best? Second, be prepared to listen (v. 1). A mother said to her teenage son, "Did you listen to the sermon this morning?" And he answered, "I didn't know you are supposed to listen." Qoheleth says it is better to be a careful listener than a careless sacrificer. Doubtless he was referring to those occasions when the Law was read to the worshipers. Inattention, or worse, idle chatter, is an offense to God (v. 2). This passage reflects a prophetic note in its admonition against careless and indifferent worship. See Amos 4:4-5; 5:21-24.

Verse 3 is a proverb of comparison, and it states that just as too intense a concentration on business affairs gives one nightmares, so too much talk results in speaking a lot of nonsense. A person who talks all the time is most likely not saying a whole lot. This proverb reminds us of the Book of Proverbs, where idle speech is denounced.

Verses 4-7 are a natural conclusion from the two previous admonitions: about worship, and about careless speech. This admonition puts the two together. When you have made a religious vow, pay it on time. We might substitute the word *pledge* for vow. When you have made a pledge to the church budget, pay it, for it is worse to pledge and not pay than not to pledge. Verse 6 warns against letting your mouth lead you into sin by making promises you do not intend to keep, and then lying about it when the "messenger" (probably a representative of the Temple) comes to collect what you promised to pay. When that person asks you to fulfill your pledge do not say, "I was only joking; it was a mistake." Verse 7 is a variation of verse 3 concerning too great a preoccupation with business and too much talk.

The Folly of Riches (5:8-20)

The basic philosophy of Qoheleth is nowhere more clearly expressed than in this passage on the folly of pursuing wealth. He sees four reasons why pursuit of wealth is a poor investment of one's energy: (1) pursuit of wealth leads to exploitation of the powerless (vv. 8-9); (2) wealth does not satisfy but instead increases anxiety (vv. 10-12); (3) wealth is transient, and those who have it today may experience poverty tomorrow (vv. 13-17); (4) therefore, the wise use of life is the enjoyment of the simple things which God provides (vv. 18-20).

Verses 8-9 state that one should not be surprised to see oppression and exploitation by the powerful and wealthy. That is the way the game is played. Every oppressor who gouges the poor fellow below him has a superior who is putting the pressure upon him. Thus, between the top and the bottom of the social heap there is a whole series of intermediate bureaucrats, each one skimming off a little of the gravy for himself, until the bottom is reached where stands the fellow who makes the gravy. This is the system which Qoheleth deplores in verse 8. Jesus also recognized and deplored it (Matt. 20:25). Verse 9 is difficult because the text is not clear. The RSV translates in a manner that puts Qoheleth on the side of kings, making him say that, though there is injustice and oppression in the system, it is better to have someone in charge (the king) than to let every person do as he pleases. If no one is there to enforce the regulations, things become disorderly and disintegration sets in. "Cultivated fields" certainly represents an ordered, developed society. It is the age-old argument for the necessity of law and order. However, this verse has been alternately translated to put Qoheleth in the camp of those who doubt the value of kings: "[The real wealth of a country is in its cultivated land]" (AB), and thus by implication, not in its king. In either case, wealth tends to engender oppression and exploitation of the weak by the wealthy. Qoheleth may be admitting that such a condition is necessary to the preservation of a state, but he says that it is one of the problems with wealth.

The second admonition concerning the pursuit of riches is in verses 10-12. Money has no power to satisfy; rather, it is like salt water when drunk by a thirsty person. The more one drinks the thirstier one becomes. Verse 11 says that as your wealth increases so do your responsibilities ("they increase who eat them"). What advantage has all this wealth, anyway? What satisfaction does the rich man get from counting his money? When he has more than he can possibly use, it only serves the vanity of his eyes (v. 11b). Further, the laborer sleeps well at night, whether he has eaten at a table groaning with food, or has had a simple supper of bread and cheese. In fact, he will probably sleep better if he has not overeaten. The rich and powerful person, however, will not sleep well. He has consistently overindulged and punished his body with food from all his resources. He digs his grave with his teeth. We Americans have been doing that for a long time, while most of the rest of the world stands around and watches us as they chew on a crust of bread.

Verses 13-17 constitute the third warning about pursuit of money. What if you fight, claw, and maneuver yourself to the top, only to take a nasty fall back to the bottom? That story has been written many times. Moreover, there is a sense in which it happens to the rich man every time. He cannot take it with him. He came from his mother's womb naked, and he returns to the dust in precisely the same condition (v. 16). "How much did he leave?" was asked about a recently-deceased rich man. "He left it all," was the answer. Seeing that riches are transient, and that we cannot avoid some bad effects from wealth, it is vain to run over your brothers and sisters and kill yourself trying to accumulate.

The final word of Qoheleth in this section is a positive one about how to live one's life (vv. 18-20). These verses show that Qoheleth is not a revolutionist who opposes the powerful and the wealthy simply because they are powerful and wealthy. Rather, he does not see power and wealth as ends in themselves. They are means toward the enjoyment of life, means which God has provided for certain persons. Qoheleth's philosophy is that one should learn to appreciate and enjoy whatever one has, whatever one's lot in life. Qoheleth is certainly no advocate of social reform, as he is committed to a doctrine of God's ordering everyone to be in whatever place he has put them. In this system, there is no hope of upward mobility.

Hopes and Desires Ultimately Frustrated (6:1-12)

Chapter 6 further elaborates the thoughts set forth at the end of chapter 5. He has recognized that God gives some men power and wealth, and he sees a certain determinism about our common existence. God has ordained that some should be poor and others rich, and Qoheleth believes that both rich and poor should accept their lot without complaint or pride.

But in chapter 6 he takes the matter a step further. Being rich is not in itself a boon. The real blessing is to be able to enjoy whatever is your lot. If God withholds from the rich man the ability to enjoy life—by giving him poor health, a bad attitude, or some other type of affliction—he is to be pitied, no matter how rich he is. Everyone has seen rich people who answer to this description. Such a person knows only how to work as though he were a slave. He accumulates wealth but it never helps him, and after he is gone some stranger (perhaps a distant relative, an unknown heir, a successor to the rich man's business?) enjoys what he gave his life to accumulate. To live like that is vanity, and a source of grief (v. 2).

Verse 3 goes further in Qoheleth's defense of the enjoyment of life as the highest good. Two blessings were considered as being of measureless worth—to have many children and to live a long time. Qoheleth is perhaps engaging in a bit of exaggeration in order to stress his point. He says that having a hundred children and living a long life are both empty achievements if one does not enjoy his life while he lives it. "And also has no burial" (v. 3c) appears to have been displaced in the text and is treated as such by many translators. It fits better with the saying about the "untimely birth," the miscarriage. For the stillborn fetus no provision was made for a formal burial. Burial was an important religious rite, and certainly a man with many sons would expect to be buried properly. But a miscarriage would not. Qoheleth once again is stating his case in extreme terms. He argues that the stillborn fetus which never had opportunity to know the good things of this life is better off than the man who had access to them but never knew how to enjoy them (vv. 4-5). Again, long life (even a thousand years twice over!) is not in itself enough to make life worthwhile. Not quantity, but quality counts with Qoheleth. What good is there in many years? When you are dead, you are dead (v. 6b), and you head for the place where all the dead reside—the place of nothingness.

Verses 7-9 further emphasize the worthlessness of those things customarily considered to be virtues. For example, what is the value of toil? A man who has to work for his bread never gets ahead, Qoheleth argues. He just works to put food on the table, but the appetite is not permanently satisfied, only temporarily stilled. Tomorrow he will be hungry again, and so it will go as long as he lives—he works to eat and eats to work. Again, Qoheleth sees little long-range advantage of the wise over the foolish. When both are dead, will it matter? The same is true of the poor man who tries to conduct himself properly in life (v. 8). What, in the long run, has he gained? The implied answer is plainly, nothing.

Verse 9 restates the basic tenet of Qoheleth's philosophy: "Enjoy what you are given." What is tangible ("the sight of the eyes") is preferable to will-o'-the-wisp desires—"A bird in the hand," and so on.

The statement on the disappointment of hopes and desires concludes in verses 10-12. Here the writer asserts again the deterministic nature of the universe. What has come to be is preordered and prearranged. Man has no power to alter the circumstances in which he has been put because the one who put him there (God) is stronger than man (v. 10b). To waste words talking about it is to indulge in vain and idle nonsense. The more one talks, the more useless it is; it is totally profitless to man (v. 11).

The reason is that we are all locked into a system. We are a part of that system. We cannot tell what is best for us, because our perspective is much too limited. We know nothing of the nature of the life before or after us. All we know is now, and if we fail to make the most of now we have lost it all (v. 12).

Relativism and Moderation (7:1-22)

Qoheleth's view of the universe is that God is Creator and Orderer of life, but that he is remote. God is not involved in the sort of continual dialogue spoken of by the prophets. Instead, God is removed, and above man's struggle. God has ordained man's lot, but he is not a participant with man in such a way as would make it possible for man to change anything in the scheme of the universe. All man can do is arrange his own life in such a way as to get the most out of what has been allotted him.

But this is not to say that Qoheleth sees no value in moral striving, or that he does not believe in virtue. There are relative goods to be sought after. Verses 1-22 names and comments on several of these. They are in the form of seven proverbs, about each of which Qoheleth adds his own comments.

Verse 1 celebrates the value of a good reputation. Here there is a clever and memorable play on words. In Hebrew "name" is *shem*, while "ointment" is *shemen*. The value of such a literary device is obvious. Ointment was used both at the time of birth and death. The reason that the day of death is to be chosen over the day of birth is that the newborn has had no opportunity to earn a good name, but if the man on his deathbed has maintained the good opinion of those who know him, he is truly blessed.

In the second proverb of comparison (v. 2), where one thing is cited as better than another, Qoheleth continues his thoughts about the value of having reached the day of one's death with an unsullied name. Here he argues that it is better to go to a house of mourning than to the house of feasting. Why that unexpected reversal of customary judgment? Most of us would much prefer a festival to a funeral. Qoheleth argues that the funeral is much more significant, for it is the universal lot of all who are born, while feasting is an occasional and sometime thing. The "house of mourning" tends to cause those who visit to think sober thoughts about the meaning of life, while the feast may allow one to avoid the very things one should be thinking about.

Verse 3 is another of the proverbs which by their unexpected claim attract attention and make one think. Who would defend sorrow as better than laughter? Qoheleth quotes a proverb which avows that as true. How so? The answer lies along the lines seen in verse 2: Though one may have many occasions of laughter, one meets death personally only once. "The heart is made glad" (v. 3b) indicates that despite the sober occasion of sorrow, it is good for the mind (heart) to have to come to terms with the fact of death and its meaning. That this is Qoheleth's meaning is made more explicit by verse 4, in which it is plainly said that the wise person's mind is occupied with the ultimate adventure of dying, while the fool is interested primarily in amusement. He has no time or inclination to consider the certainty of his death.

Verses 5-6 go together and are the more effective because of the use of alliteration. This four-line proverb is an admonition not to listen to fools who know only loud, brash talk and laughter. Rebuke from the wise is to be preferred to the song (Hebrew, *shir*) of fools (v. 5), for the laughter of fools is as empty and worthless as burning thorns (Hebrew, *sirim*) under a pot (Hebrew, *sir*). One does not get much accomplished building a fire of thornbushes; neither can a fool's empty and senseless carryings-on be of much help to us. Seek, instead, the wise man's rebuke.

But it is difficult to follow the course of wisdom (v. 7). Obstacles strew wisdom's path. One is oppression. Persecution has a way of testing us. So does bribery. On the one hand the wise may be oppressed into capitulating; on the other he may be tempted by a bribe to sell out.

Verse 8 suggests a similar thought to that of verse 1. How a thing comes out is much more important than how it begins. Thus the person who takes the long view and is willing to wait for delayed gratification is better than the one who demands immediate results. Patience is preferable to pride of spirit (v. 8b). See 1 Kings 20:11 for a vivid proverb making the same point.

Verse 9 is a similar admonition to the observation of verse 8. Qoheleth is here admonishing against being quick-tempered, saying that such behavior has its normal dwelling place in the heart of fools. Wise people control their tempers.

Some questions are inappropriate for the wise person. One is, "Why aren't things as good as in the good old days?" Why is this question inappropriate? Because, says Qoheleth, God ordains each time to be what it is, and it could not be other than the way God has ordained it. To complain of your own time is to rail against God. Besides, all time is cyclical, according to Qoheleth. What has been will be. If you find yourself in a dark moment of history, that is just the way it is. It is your lot to live in this particular period and not complain (v. 10).

Verses 11-12 are plainly a bit elitist and aristocratic. Qoheleth is saying here that there are two great assets in the search for a pleasant existence—money and wisdom. To be born with a generous inheritance is made much better by the acquisition of wisdom. Wise and poor is better than rich and foolish, but wise and rich is best.

Verse 13 restates the doctrine of the immutability of life. What God has arranged, man cannot rearrange. See 1:15; 3:15; 6:10. Verse 14 concludes the thought of absolute predestination by saying that not only is it impossible for man to change God's arrangement of the world, it is equally impossible for him to understand the whys and wherefores of the arrangement. One should accept whatever is one's lot, whether prosperity or adversity, without asking "Why?"—for one can get no answer. It is simply the way things are. See 3:11.

Verses 15-22 advise moderation in all things, in the light of the realities noted above: God allots a time and place for everything; man can only do his best in his time and place without hope of altering anything, or even of understanding it. Life is full of mystery—righteous people perishing before their time in their righteousness, while wicked people live out long lives in wickedness (v. 15). Such things ought not to be, but are. What is the wise person to do? Be moderate (vv. 16-18). Don't be too righteous or too wicked, too wise or too much of a fool. Extremes are bad. They may lead you into destroying yourself, and to an early death. The saint and the criminal may wind up on adjoining scaffolds. Thus the general principle is, "Take this and take that," a moderate amount of one thing and a moderate amount of its counterpart (v. 18). If you do that you will come out all right (v. 18b).

Verse 19 strikes again the familiar theme of the supreme worth of wisdom, but verse 20 takes the thought a step further by saying that no one is wise and righteous all the time, never sinning. This verse reminds us of Paul's statements about the universality of sin (see Rom. 3). The point relates to the doctrine of moderation. In effect, Qoheleth says, "Relax; don't take yourself too seriously. No matter how wise and righteous you are, you are not perfect." If you begin to take yourself too seriously, just remember that not everybody thinks you are simply dandy. Don't let yourself take too seriously what others say about you, either. If you listen to everybody who mentions your name, you may hear, even from your servant, some things you do not want to hear. He may praise you to your face, but what do you suppose he says to your back? (v. 21). Are you shocked by the suggestion that some people may curse you? Haven't you often been guilty of cursing others? (v. 22). So, here is a doctrine of moderation about all things, especially about oneself. Don't take yourself too seriously, or imagine that you are either better or worse than you are. Actually, we are pretty ordinary people, and most of us are more alike the rest of us than we care to admit to ourselves. In all of us there is good and bad is Qoheleth's teaching.

"A Good Man Is Hard to Find" (7:23-29)

The concluding paragraph of chapter 7 is a confession of the impossibility of arriving at complete wisdom. All one can do is struggle with the issues of life, recognizing that they are ultimately beyond man's comprehension. "All this" (v. 23a) means what the author is about to say. The conclusions he announces were not rashly arrived at, but were the result of applying his mind diligently. He set out to be wise, but found it an elusive goal, "far from me" (v. 23c). Verse 24 expands upon the unattainability of ultimate wisdom, which is the sense of verse 23. It is not only far off, but very deep. In his search for "the sum of things" (v. 25b), Qoheleth came to one certain conclusion: Wickedness is folly, and foolishness is madness (stupidity) (v. 25c). Qoheleth may be unable to define wisdom precisely, but he can say something specific about its opposite, folly. Folly is wickedness. As Job 28:28 says, "To depart from evil is understanding."

Although Qoheleth cannot define the boundaries of wisdom, there are some things about it that he can delineate. One of them has been noted —wickedness is not wisdom. Another example of the lack of wisdom is becoming ensnared by a scheming woman (v. 26). The sexism of the Wisdom writers is manifest, and there is no way wholly to dismiss it. Proverbs, to be sure, regards a good woman as a great benediction upon a man's life (see ch. 31), but there is no doubt but that the Wisdom teachers believed that woman is one of the chief sources of man's defection from God. A great deal is written by them warning against the enticements of the designing woman but nothing warning the woman against the designs of the evil man. Of course, it must be recognized that the teachers did not teach girls, only young men, the girls being taught by their mothers at home. Suffice it to say, the teachers who wrote the Wisdom Literature were deeply concerned about the power of sexual temptation to destroy a young man's desire to know God.

Verse 27 reiterates the diligent search of the "Preacher" to know God's secrets of life, but he confesses in verse 28 that he has been compelled to be satisfied with only bits and pieces of wisdom. The heart of it is, "I have not found." On the basis of his limited knowledge, he can announce that a good man is hard to find, "one man among a thousand" (v. 28*b*), but in his experience no such woman has been found. What he did find is that God made man good, but man has "sought out many devices" (v. 29) by which to defect from God's good purpose. The word used for "devices" in Hebrew is a play on words with the word for *reason*, suggesting that man has taken the very capacity to know God through his God-given reason and corrupted it into a means of organizing life apart from God.

Learning to Be Practical About Life (8:1-9)

If, as Qoheleth has claimed in chapter 7, all wisdom and knowledge are partial, what is one to do? First, recognize that wisdom is still preferable to folly. Verse 1 of this chapter celebrates the value of wisdom. We may not know all the secrets of the universe, but that fact does not suggest the conclusion that wisdom is of no account. "Wisdom makes his face shine," that is, it is a transforming quality in one's life.

Verses 2-9 commend the practice of practicality. "To get along you must be willing to go along." Some things are unavoidable, so do not destroy yourself seeking to escape them. A case in point is the subject's relationship with the king, or translated into contemporary language, with the government. Qoheleth advises respect of and obedience to the king (v. 2). Don't go on resisting just because the duty you are ordered to carry out is "unpleasant" (v. 3*b*), for the king does as he pleases and you cannot successfully resist him. Verse 4 amplifies the king's supremacy.

The arrangement of human affairs in governments is seen by Qoheleth to be one part of the totality of God's established order in the world. Just as you cannot resist the irresistible (the king's power), so you cannot resist the day of your death (vv. 5-8). If you do right you will suffer no harm (v. 5). Everything has its appointed time (v. 6), although some of that time may be pain and misery (v. 6b). If so, that, too, has been ordained, and man must be willing to accept his lot even though trouble lies heavy upon him. The best he can do is to handle as best he can what he experiences moment by moment, for the future is hidden from his eyes (v. 7). Nobody can read the future for us. Nobody has the power to keep himself alive one breath beyond God's will for him to breathe (v. 8a). War, an historic calamity among peoples, is a part—although a terrible part—of the real world in which we are set to live. No wickedness or scheme of man will alter the way God has ordered things to be (v. 8b). Such thoughts about the way things are do not exactly qualify as sanguine. They are somber. Qoheleth was not clapping his hands with glee when he announced these conclusions. He was saying that as he understood life this is the way it is (v. 9). He does not applaud the fact that "man lords it over man to his hurt"; but that is what happens, and the wise man will accept that reality and adjust to it. One must say that total acquiescence to the status quo, such as Qoheleth seems to recommend, would rule out the revolutions and rebellions of history by which oppression has been destroyed.

The Hiddenness of God's Moral Purpose in History (8:10-17)

One recurring theme in Ecclesiastes is the mystery of God's purpose. God is so far removed from our human scene that we are left largely on our own. Inequities exist, and Qoheleth cannot understand why God allows that to happen. He believes deep in his heart that goodness is better than evil, but he sees so much evidence to suggest that it does not matter whether one is good or evil that he confesses to being confused. His ultimate reliance is upon God's wisdom and God's right to run the universe as he chooses, and upon man's right to enjoy the everyday and ordinary good things. That is the sense of the language in verses 10-17.

Verse 10 is a commentary on the apparent inequity of wickedness going unreckoned and unpunished. Picture the wicked, powerful community leader's funeral. Everybody in town turns out, and there is a big display of admiration, although everybody knows that he was a scoundrel. The preacher cooperates in the charade by saying words of praise over the dead man's coffin, and "preaches him into heaven." Such persons in their lifetime were praised in the city, and they went "in and out of the holy place." They were regularly seen in the right places. But most people knew what they had done to exploit and wrong those weaker than themselves.

Verse 11 is a kind of protest against the way things are and a reminder to God that he would get better results if he punished the offender "speedily." Because people seem to get away with doing wrong without any adverse consequences, others are encouraged to do wrong, too. If it takes three years to bring an accused criminal to trial, then another two years to run the course of all his legal appeals before he is finally put in jail, it is easy to see why people do not fear being apprehended for criminal behavior.

Verses 12-13 show the inner workings of Qoheleth's mind and heart. He observes the inequities of life, and how the wicked appear to suffer no ill consequences, yet he cannot get the consent of his mind and heart to settle for that. If the world is not to be a chaotic funny farm, there must be some system of reward and punishment. Otherwise, nothing makes sense. Therefore, Qoheleth says that, though he cannot explain it on the basis of evidence, he nonetheless believes that it will be well with "those who fear God," and not well with those who flaunt him.

One sees Qoheleth talking with himself in this passage as clearly as anywhere in Ecclesiastes. Verse 14 returns to the problem of inequity which can only be surmounted by faith, not by reason. God's moral order—if there is one—seems not to operate with consistency. Some people who deserve good get evil, and some who are notoriously wicked appear to enjoy the rewards that ought to go to the righteous. What can one say about such realities? Only this: "Vanity." It simply should not be.

Verse 15 puts Qoheleth back into his usual mind-set, in which he declares that man must learn to enjoy the simple pleasures of life and stop trying to figure out transcendent and eternal matters, inasmuch as such mysteries are hidden from his eyes. The small pleasures which can be enjoyed daily will go with a man all his days, while the ultimate matters are beyond man's comprehension. Verses 16-17 reiterate one of Qoheleth's major conclusions, the one stated in verses 14-15. No matter how hard you try; even if you worked on the problem day and night, not even taking time out to sleep (v. 16b), it would not matter. Study the ways of God with all your might, yet you still cannot discern them. Even if a wise man claims that he knows the ways of God, don't believe him. No man knows.

The Common Fate of Death (9:1-18)

Since no man knows and understands the ways of God, we are driven back upon our faith. What kind of God is God? Can he be trusted? Qoheleth believes that God can, but he admits that there is mystery beyond our understanding. The deeds of the wise and righteous are in God's hands. Is God's response to what man offers love or hate (v. 1b)? Man cannot be sure because he simply does not know. The past offers no clue to Qoheleth. All that went before is vanity (v. 1c). The problem as far as Qoheleth can understand it is that all life comes to the same conclusion, death and Sheol. "One fate comes to all" (v. 2a), and Qoheleth then lists six pairs of opposites. How could such opposites have the same end? They do, as Qoheleth fears, because death is the end. Life is not much to glory in, inasmuch as man is morally weak and mentally unstable ("hearts . . . full of evil, and madness is in their hearts")—and death is the inescapable consequence (v. 3).

Even so, life is to be preferred over death, for the living at the least have life (and where there is life there is hope), while the dead have nothing (v. 4a). Then Qoheleth quotes a proverb: "A living dog is better than a dead lion." The point is that the dog was not considered by the Hebrews to be an admirable animal. He was thought of much as we think of the wild hyena. He was a scavenger, not a pet, and was considered unclean. The lion might be wild and ferocious, but he was considered to be an awe-inspiring beast, the king of beasts. Nonetheless, given the choice of being a live dog or a dead lion, grab the first choice (v. 4b).

The living may live with the somber realization that death is the end they have to look forward to, but the dead don't even have that feeling —they have no feeling at all, and they have nothing to dread or to anticipate. There is no more reward to hope for, not even that they will be remembered, for the memory of the dead is short-lived (v. 5). This is a sobering and important lesson to learn. If this life is all there is, we are as Paul said in 1 Corinthians 15:19 of all men most to be pitied. What makes man's lot dread-producing is that he knows he must die. If he has no hope beyond the event of death, he has reason to share Qoheleth's somberness. Verse 6 is an eloquent statement of the hopelessness of death without the anticipation of any more life. Love, hate, and envy— all the common emotions of human beings in this life—are gone forever if death is all, and those who have died "have no more for ever any share" in the life we know (v. 6b) here upon this good earth.

What should one do, being convinced that death is the end? Qoheleth returns to one of his major themes: Live today, enjoy the simple pleasures, eat your bread, and drink your wine with a merry heart. Why? Because God has already approved whatever you do (v. 7b). It is almost as though Qoheleth is saying that God does not care one way or another. God is remote, and he is not going to reward you or punish you, whatever you do, so you might as well do what gives you joy for the moment.

White garments (v. 8a) and oil on the head (v. 8b) were both symbols of enjoyment and leisure. Qoheleth is in tune with his own philosophy of life: Don't take yourself too seriously; relax and have some fun. Come to the party. Don't be so grim. We would say, "Put on your Sunday dress or suit." Look your best; act as if you are having a celebration.

Verse 9 is in form of a proverb which adds a dimension to Qoheleth's recommendations about living the good life. Here the wholesomeness of marital love is recognized. Remember that the writer is addressing young men, and that is why he talks about the "wife whom you love," instead of "spouse." The Old Testament plainly supports marriage and the family and does not endorse a celibate life as superior to the married state. On the contrary, Qoheleth is reflecting the faith of his fathers when he admonishes the young men whom he advises to enjoy fully their marriages, for that is God's intention. It is part of God's plan for man.

Verse 10 is the ultimate statement of "seize the day." Don't be half-hearted about the task at hand. Wherever you are, be all there. Give it your best shot, no matter whether the assignment seems challenging or not. Why? Because that is the only "shot" you have at life—the one at hand. In the state of death (Sheol) all the things which mark you as human—work, thought, knowledge, and wisdom—are nonexistent. Christians must consider how far it is from Qoheleth to the resurrection of our Lord Jesus Christ.

Not only is death the great equalizer, but also life, as Qoheleth observes it, does not afford any reason to believe that effort is always rewarded. That is the meaning of verse 11. The fastest runner does not always win the race; the strongest army does not always win the battle; the wise and the intelligent do not always wind up with the rewards of material goods; nor does recognition ("favor") always come to the most skillful. Instead, "time"—the passing days and years—and "chance"—what simply happens to us in the course of living the passing years—happens to all. As Qoheleth sees it, there is an inescapable haphazardness in life. We are victims, he goes on to say in verse 12, like fish caught in a net and birds trapped in a snare. Thus, at a totally unexpected moment, the net closes around us, the snare is tripped, and we are captured by a circumstance we never anticipated.

Verse 13 introduces a parable which is told in verses 14-15. It is about a poor, wise man who was able by his wisdom to save his city under seige by a great king. Yet when the seige was broken, he was promptly forgotten. Doubtless some general or bureaucrat took credit for saving the city! Qoheleth finds that sort of unjust thing happening too often in life. Nonetheless, wisdom is still the summum bonum, the highest of all human gifts, and certainly to be chosen above power, even if it is despised (v. 16). Indeed, the quiet words of the wise (doubtless spoken in the relatively noiseless classroom) are better than the ravings of a ruler whose subjects are fools who cheer whatever he says, no matter how illogical and untrue (v. 17). Verse 18 again commends wisdom in the context of the discussion of power and warfare, arguing that wisdom is a better weapon than implements of warfare, yet recognizing that much of the good done by the wise may be undone by a sinner. This verse should be taken as a reminder of the influence for good or evil of a single person.

A Teacher's Notebook (10:1 to 11:8)

Someone has entitled the section listed on the line immediately above, "A Teacher's Notebook," visualizing the collection of sayings in this section as brief, cryptic notes from which the teacher was lecturing. The seemingly disconnected sayings which are found in this part of Ecclesiastes could indeed have been the bases for amplification in instruction of the teacher's pupils. Whatever they were in the beginning, they are now a collection of wise sayings concerning a variety of observations about life.

In the first proverb, a comparison is made between the disagreeable odor caused by dead flies in otherwise sweet-smelling ointment and the power of a little folly to spoil a great amount of wisdom and honor (v. 1). The ointment, being sweet-smelling, would attract flies, as would honey. But flies in your honey would not be pleasant! So the deleterious effects of folly in a batch of wisdom.

Verse 2 interestingly enough identifies right and left with good and evil, respectively. Jesus used the same figure in his parable of the last judgment (see Matt. 25:33).

Verse 3 is a jibe at the foolish person who, even though he attempts to walk "on the road," that is, in the "straight and narrow path," makes a fool of himself. His very demeanor proclaims to the world, "Here is a fool."

Verses 4-7 belong together, for they are a brief discussion of the etiquette of the youth preparing to serve the king in his court. The young men who were in the wise teacher's classroom were doubtless preparing for some branch of government service, as the wise were used as advisers to the government, and as recorders of its records. How do you "go along to get along"? One thing is this: If the king is angry with you, lie low; don't make any rash moves to leave your place. If you defer to the angry king, even though you may know that you have done nothing to deserve his disfavor, his anger will go away (v. 4). Soon he will have something else to be upset about! Verse 5 recognizes that rulers are not infallible. As likely as not, the king's anger is unjustified. Many a fool occupies a king's throne, while some who are worthy and wise (and their wealth attests that they have God's favor) occupy places of low estate (v. 6). Indeed, in this mixed-up world, slaves sometimes are honored by being put on horses (a sign of power and prestige), while princes have to walk like slaves. In other words, the world is often upside down and makes no logical sense (v. 7).

Verses 8-11 are all about a single truth, namely, every gain in life involves risktaking, and in about every worthwhile endeavor there is the possibility of disaster. There are always consequences, and sometimes they surprise and injure us. Thus, verse 8 says that if you dig a pit you may be the one who falls into it, instead of the person whom you hoped to trap. Like Haman in the Book of Esther, you may hang from the gallows you erected for Mordecai. Another metaphor in verse 8b tells the same thing. If you go around digging through walls (possibly to rob the house of which the wall is a part, or to sneak inside a walled town) you may get bitten by a snake who has made his home in the wall. Or if you quarry stones (v. 9) you could be crushed by the very stones you dig out. If you split logs be careful how you do it, for one may fly up and hit you (v. 9b). And if your axe is dulled you ought to sharpen it, otherwise you will have to exert more and yet more energy to get the wood cut (v. 10). Finally, there is no use to summon the snake charmer after the snake has already bitten somebody (v. 11). That is like locking the barn door after the horse has been stolen. So, take due precautions about whatever you do.

Verses 12-15 contrast the way of the wise and the fool, as seen particularly in what their speech reveals. A wise man's speech commends him to others, while a fool's lips "eat him up" (v. 12, AT). The more words coming out of his mouth the less impressive he reveals himself to be. It is as though he gradually devours himself before his auditors, until there is nothing left but a big mouth! Verse 13 extends the metaphor of the fool's words. There is a cumulative effect in what he says. It begins as folly and ends as wickedness and madness. The fool "runs on at the mouth"; he "multiplies words" (v. 14a). He shows no restraint, the sort of restraint shown by the wise who know their limitations in being able to tell what is to come. The fool knows no such limits. He is the resident expert on every subject! Verse 15 is troublesome. The two parts of the proverb do not seem to fit. The first part is understandable—the fool wears himself out (as well as wearing everybody else out). The second part also is understandable—the fool "can't find his way to town" (AT), perhaps the ultimate disparagement.

Verses 16-17 are a pair belonging together, and contrasting the lot of the land which has a simpleton ("child") for a king (v. 16) with that of the land which has a king who has risen to the position because of his own merit ("the son of free men," v. 17). In the first, the lack of leadership will allow the kind of disintegration of the court in which the "princes" (chief officers) "party" all day ("in the morning") rather than doing their work. In the second, the princes have their meals at the proper time, and because they are hungry and need to eat, and not because they want to carouse and get drunk. A strong leader makes for an orderly government.

Verse 18 is a proverb familiar to the readers of the Book of Proverbs. It deplores laziness and indolence. The lazy man does not repair his leaky roof when it is not raining because he does not need to do so then, and when it is raining he cannot. Extended, the proverb means that laziness is a disintegrating and evil force.

Verse 19 is a candid if not somewhat cynical statement about the power of money to get what people value. It says that while the simple pleasures of bread and wine are nice to have and bring enjoyment to one's days, one has to have money to get along, even to pay for the bread and wine. "Money answers everything" is a maxim one would not expect to hear from Jesus.

Discretion is the subject of verse 20. Don't utter a word against those who can damage you, such as the king or some rich person. Don't even think such thoughts in your mind or whisper them in the privacy of your bedroom. It is amazing how news gets around. If you don't want a thing repeated, don't say it. The "bird of the air" or "some winged creature" reflects the humor of the writer of this proverb.

Ecclesiastes 11:1-2 recommends a prudential pattern of living. "Cast your bread upon the waters" is a metaphor for doing good deeds. The promise is that if you help others your kindness will be returned to you. Verse 2 says essentially the same thing, in a different form. Share with "seven," or "even to eight," probably means to put no limits upon your willingness to help others. Seven was the number of totality or completeness. Eight must, therefore, be considered a way of saying, "Go to the limit, and then go a little bit further." The reason for such generosity is that you never know when you are going to need help yourself. The pragmatism of such admonitions to generosity should trouble us. It is one thing to recognize that doing good may make friends who will help us when we need them, but it is another to commend doing good on pragmatic grounds.

Verse 3 is a vivid statement of Qoheleth's belief concerning the inevitability of events. What is to be will be. Full clouds empty themselves in a rain. A fallen tree falls one way or the other; it cannot fall both ways, or beginning to fall one way, change its direction. There is a certain inevitability about life.

Verse 4 is another occasional proverb, not particularly related to those with which it appears. This is a metaphor concerning the tactics of the overly-cautious person. He is always surveying the wind at sowing season lest the wind be so high that his seed is blown away. He waits for perfect conditions and they never seem quite right, so he doesn't sow at all. Likewise, at harvest season he wants to be sure not to cut his grain and have rain upon it, so he waits to harvest until he is sure there is no chance of rain. He never gets around to harvesting his crop.

Verse 5 is another statement of the mystery of life. You have to act without full knowledge of everything. The mystery of human reproduction, or how a fetus in a womb becomes a person, is an example of our condition about much of life. We cannot understand the work of God, but we cannot cease to function even though we do not know everything. Verse 6 complements verse 5. Inasmuch as we do not know what is best to do, do all the good you can in the confidence that some of it will produce a harvest. It is like a man sowing his field. Who knows whether sowing in the morning or in the evening is preferable? Sometimes it is better one way, and sometimes another. The object is to sow when you can, and leave the results to the forces beyond your control.

Verses 7-8 reiterate Qoheleth's view that life is very precious. The figures of light and darkness represent life and death. To enjoy the sweet light of the sun is pleasant, and one should savor it, remembering that "the days of darkness (death) will be many." The ultimate meaning of life eludes Qoheleth. He declares it vain.

Remember! (11:9 to 12:8)

This passage is perhaps the best known in Ecclesiastes, although its meaning is often misinterpreted. From the verses just ahead of this section, it is clear that Qoheleth believes that life is to be cherished and enjoyed. Such sentiments are also consistent with his entire framework. Apparently he is himself in the sunset years of his life, and he is writing to youth who have their lives ahead of them. Do they know how fortunate they are to be young? The admonition is: "Rejoice, . . . do (walk) what your heart (mind) and your eyes desire you to do. But remember, judgment day is coming, so do not ignore God's judgment, and order your life by these two principles: what you want to do and what is consistent with God's will" (v. 9, AT). Further, avoid mental anguish and physical pain (v. 10)—for "you are only young once," and youth is fleeting. It soon passes, so enjoy it.

In 12:1 we have perhaps the best-known verse in Ecclesiastes, and perhaps one of the most misused texts of the Bible. From what we have seen of Qoheleth's thought, it is clear that the focus is upon the need to make the most of your youth, the salad days of life, because it all too soon passes away. Perhaps the admonition "Remember your Creator" is the correct translation of the Hebrew text. If so, Qoheleth is saying, "Don't forget that while you are enjoying your youthful living you need also to remember God." That is quite possible as a translation. However, some translators believe that "Creator" here should be translated "grave," causing the writer to say, "Remember during your youth that one day you are going to die" (AT). Some young people seem to believe that they are immortal. That may be one reason why so many have fatal accidents. They are careless because they do not believe it can happen to them.

Whichever is the better translation, the sense of the passage is that old age will come quicker than you can imagine. As you grow older, the birthdays begin to fly by.

In a series of beautiful metaphors, Qoheleth describes the infirmities and failures of old age. Old age is the winter of life: the warmth of the sun is gone; the rains of winter come; and clouds return even after rain to cast a gloomy haze over everything (v. 2). The trembling "keepers of the house" are the hands; the "strong men" are the legs; the "grinders" are the teeth; the dimmed lookers are the eyes (v. 3). "Doors on the street" are ears, and "grinding is low" refers to poor hearing. The one who "rises up at the voice of a bird" is the elderly person who is no longer able to sleep late, and he cannot hear singing any more (v. 4). "Afraid also of what is high" reflects the fear of falling and breaking a limb. Indeed, they are afraid of many unknown hazards. The "almond tree" is an allusion to the white hair of the elderly. The grasshopper dragging itself along is the picture of the old person who has been crippled by a stroke. Failing desire is a reference to the receding sexuality of the aged (c. 5b). The "eternal home" to which man goes at death does not indicate that Qoheleth believes in heaven, but is instead a poetic expression of the Hebrew belief that death is final. The "mourners go about the streets," that is, they resume life after the funeral for the elderly deceased one (v. 5c). The silver cord, the golden bowl, the pitcher, and the wheel all refer to the ending of life with the event of death (v. 6). Verse 7 is not a Greek suggestion about body and soul being separated at death, the soul surviving the event of dying. It is rather consistent with Hebraic thought that man returns to dust (ceases to exist) and the breath of life (spirit) which God breathed into him at his creation goes back to God. (See Job 34:14-15.) Ecclesiastes really ends with verse 8, where the theme announced in the beginning is repeated, now with the confidence that the thesis has been substantiated by the evidence Qoheleth has presented.

Appendix (12:9-14)

Verses 9-10 add a personal biographical note to the book. The Preacher was a teacher, *hakham*, one who made his living by teaching young men. He was also a student and collector and arranger of the wise sayings, the proverbs, of his people. He did his work with utmost care. He did not sacrifice his integrity in his work, but did it "uprightly."

Verse 11 is a summary statement of the case for wisdom. The teachings of the wise serve two purposes: as goads to prod the mind of the student to think about life and its meaning, and as nails to fasten securely the great foundational truths of life. These sayings of truth incorporated in the collections of wisdom have their origin in the one true Shepherd, who is God.

Verses 12-14 bring Ecclesiastes to an end with an admonition. First, there are a great many "books," and one can study them to one's great weariness, but beware of going beyond the teachings of the wise. All necessary has been said, and the summation of it all is "Fear God and keep his commandments" (v. 13). This is the essence of wisdom. See Job 28:28. Be assured of this, God is not indifferent, no matter how things appear to us, but he will bring into judgment all we do, whether good or evil.

The Song of Solomon

Introduction

In many respects the Song of Solomon, or perhaps more accurately, Song of Songs, is one of the strangest and most difficult writings in the Bible. Even the title is unclear. The language in the ascription at the beginning of the book, "which is Solomon's," may also be translated "to Solomon," or "about Solomon," or "for Solomon." There has been disagreement across the centuries not only about authorship of the book, but about its meaning, its purpose, and even whether or not it should have been included in the canon of Scripture. The two foremost Jewish schools of thought in the first century BC disagreed on whether Song of Songs should be in the canon. The Palestinian school of Shammai, being conservative and strict constructionist, opposed its inclusion, while the school of Hillel, in Babylon, supported it. It was accepted in time, as we know, and some who had taken it to be no more than a collection of somewhat risqué love songs were strictly forbidden to use it as a drinking song at times of merriment.

When was the book written? Few scholars support the theory of Solomonic authorship. At the same time, there is widespread agreement among scholars that the book was written very early in the development of Hebrew religious thought. The book is composed of a series of love poems, often sensual and boldly erotic in nature. Many interpreters, both Jewish and Christian, conclude that the poems may have their origin in religious ritual associated with the annual fall and spring festivals of the Jewish calendar, and that these rituals, in turn, may have drawn from even earlier Canaanite religious festivals in which sexuality and fertility of the deities were ritualized and celebrated with the changing of the seasons of nature. While such pagan rites were abhorrent to Israel's prophetic figures, it is noteworthy that such noble prophets as Hosea and Jeremiah based much of their teaching concerning God's care for his people on the allegorical comparison of God with the husband or

128

father, and Israel with the bride or child. Did the love songs of the Song of Songs come out of a background of ordinary love songs which were transformed and reinterpreted allegorically to celebrate the love of God for Israel, and subsequently in Christian times, for the church? That is certainly a possibility which supports the argument for an early date for the book.

How has the book been interpreted? The interpretation that has dominated both Hebrew and Christian thought is that the book is an allegory. Such an interpretation is found in the Jewish Talmud by AD 150. The bridegroom is Yahweh, the bride is the Jewish nation, and the poems represent the continuing relationship of the two throughout Israel's history. For centuries the book was read in the public service during Passover. Today, however, it is read privately by each individual as part of the Passover celebration. Also, the allegorical interpretation of Song of Solomon has now largely been abandoned by Jewish scholarship, although it remains as the orthodox interpretation.

In Christian circles, the allegorical interpretation by which the love songs are ascribed to God and the church has persisted much longer than in Jewish circles. The bridegroom is Christ, in most Christian allegorical interpretations, and the young woman of the poems is, of course, the church. A variation of Christ as the bridegroom and the church as bride theme is one which sees the beloved of the bridegroom as the individual Christian believer. Among those who held to the Christ-church allegory of the Song of Songs were Jerome, Augustine, and John Wesley. Some Roman Catholic interpreters see the bride as the virgin Mary. Martin Luther saw the bride as the symbol of the state, and understood the poems as expressions of Solomon's gratitude to God for the loyalty of his people. Others have identified the bride of the Song with wisdom. Plainly, using the model of allegorical interpretation, the fertile imagination may discover almost limitless interpretations to the book. The allegorical interpretation, in part for that very reason, is not taken seriously today by most scholars.

Another interpretation of the Song of Songs is that it is a dramatic dialogue between two lovers. Two of the earliest Greek manuscripts of the Bible, Codex Sinaiticus and Codex Alexandrinus, even included marginal notes in the text to indicate who was speaking and who was being addressed.

Others went so far in the effort to turn the book into a dramatic dialogue that they divided the material into five acts, visualizing two char-

acters, Solomon (sometimes disguised as a shepherd) and the Shulammite woman of 6:13. Others found six acts, each with two scenes. Still
other interpreters maintained the dramatic dialogue interpretation, but
gave the book more dramatic power by interpreting three characters instead of the man and woman speaking back and forth to each other of
their love for one another. In the three-character interpretation, there
is in addition to Solomon and the Shulammite maiden a third person,
the shepherd. So the plot is about a beautiful, young, virginal, country
maiden who is loved both by the rich and powerful king and by her simple country shepherd lad. Despite the king's overtures, she remains true
to her shepherd lover. The theme thus becomes not simply the delights of
marriage, but fidelity to one's chosen.

There are certain serious problems with the three-character interpretation, perhaps the most difficult of which is that it puts Solomon in an ill-
favored light. It does not seem likely that a book being considered for
inclusion in the canon would have been accepted if that had been its true
purpose. Moreover, one must say that such interpretations rely more
upon the vivid imagination of the interpreter than the text itself, which is
a very bad precedent to set for biblical interpretation.

Another interpretation of the Song of Songs is that it was a series of
wedding songs used to celebrate the marriage of a young man and
woman. The bride and groom were hailed as a queen and king, and
their beauty and prowess in love were signaled through the songs.
Other interpreters accept the Song of Songs as simply a collection of love
songs without any deep theological meanings and not allegorical of God
and his people or Christ and the church. One of the first Christian theo-
logians to take this position, Theodore of Mopsuestia in the fourth century AD, was later anathematized by the church for doing so. Robert
Gordis, a prominent Jewish scholar, interprets Song of Songs as an
anthology of twenty-eight love poems, written over a period of five centuries from the time of Solomon to the post-Exilic Persian period.

Yet another theory of the meaning of the book is that it had its origins
in the celebration of fall and spring festivals, that the love poems were
perhaps at first related to a somewhat earthy conception of God's role in
the fertility of the earth, and that they were subsequently spiritualized
and used for a higher meaning. The Song as we now have it reflects one
of the important themes of the Old Testament, the intimate relationship
between God and his people. As noted above, the prophets were fond of
this image, and it is unthinkable that they would have used it if they

thought that it encouraged a pagan understanding of God. The marriage of Yahweh to Israel, his bride, was understood spiritually, and described the deep love which the Lord had for his people. As noted above, for centuries the Song of Songs was read during public worship on one of the days of Passover. All three annual feasts in the Jewish year, Passover-Unleavened Bread, Weeks, and Ingathering, were initially connected with seasons of the agricultural year. As has been the case with many Christian festivals, their peculiar religious significance emerged, and certain elements of the custom were given religious significance. It seems likely that the Song of Songs is just such an example. Poems or songs which might once have been thought of as only love songs came to be understood as ways of expressing allegiance to and gratitude for God. Such a theory seems to explain most easily the connection of the Song with Passover, its admission into the canon, its allegorical interpretations, and its uncertain geographical reference point. Most assuredly, it did not get into the canon simply because Solomon's name was attached to it, for other writings bearing his name were not included. If at first it was only a series of folk love songs, it must have been sacralized along the way and used within the official Hebrew liturgy of celebration of God's bountiful and saving love for his people.

What is the book's meaning for us? For one thing, it should be enjoyed for what it is—a collection of beautiful, sensuous, passionate, romantic love songs. People who are afraid of their own sensuality or who feel the need to promote asceticism will find little reason for encouragement in the Old Testament (or in the New Testament, for that matter). The Hebrews certainly devoutly believed in marital fidelity and held that the Lord commanded it. But they believed that one of God's most wonderful gifts to man and woman is the gift of love for one another. So, to begin with, enjoy the Song of Songs as a series of love poems. Remember, in the second place, that they are poetry, and poetry is the language of the emotions rather than of the reason. Poetry intends to elicit an emotional response, not a rational one. Remember, in the third place, that poetry may not be understood apart from the gift of imagination. Its fullest meanings are always concealed, and are revealed only in figure and symbol.

Did Song of Songs have its origin in secular fertility celebrations? We cannot be certain. What is certain is that this book came to be associated with some of the most powerful and beloved feelings of the Hebrew people concerning their relationship with the Lord. He was their husband, their bridegroom, and they were his bride. The poems may be read and enjoyed at either or both levels of understanding. It will be impossible to read them, however, without sensing their highly romantic, sensuous nature.

Reference has been made to the fact that the ascription does not require the language "which is Solomon's" but may be "to" or "about" Solomon. "Song of Songs" means the best of all songs.

First Speech of the Maiden (1:2-7)

The essentially romantic and physical nature of the Song is clearly indicated in the opening lines of the maiden's first speech to her beloved. She longs for "the kisses of [his] mouth," and his love is better, more intoxicating, than wine. The fragrance of the ointment (after-shave lotion?) he uses is enticingly delicious. Little wonder the maidens all love him and languish for him. Who are the maidens? Members of Solomon's harem? Votaries or priestesses attached to the sacred shrine? We would prefer to think that the reference is to "the girls," the friends of the maiden whose love is claimed by the one to whom the song is addressed. Verse 4 is a continuation of the love song of the maiden to her "king," a common address for the bridegroom. The sense of the verse is the marriage chamber, the joyous couple entering it after the public festivities celebrating their commitment to each other. "They" in 4d probably is an allusion to the maidens spoken of in verse 3.

Verses 5-6 are a self-description of the maiden of the Song. She describes herself as very dark, "swarthy" (v. 6), but "lovely" (NIV), her complexion compared to the tents of Kedar (v. 5b). Kedar was a nomadic tribe of Arabia, and its tents were made of black goats' hair. But she is also as beautiful as the curtains of Solomon's palace or perhaps the Temple. Verse 6 acknowledges that the maiden's swarthy complexion may be startling, if not even offensive, to the chorus which sings refrains in this Song of Songs. "Do not stare at me," reads a contemporary translation (NIV). The cause of her darkness is that she has been in the sun, unlike a princess who would have been sheltered in the palace, her skin kept white and fair. This maiden, beloved of her "king," has had to work in the fields as a vinedresser. Her "mother's sons" (perhaps her half-brothers? Is the maiden an early Cinderella?) had put her into the vineyards to work because they did not like her. They treated her as if she were a common hired hand. And because she had to work so hard, she was unable to tend her own vineyard, perhaps meaning that she had not been able to take care of her own personal appearance and grooming needs (v. 6b).

Verse 7 is the maiden's plea to her lover to know where he pastures his flock so that she will not have to wander about the countryside, going from flock to flock looking for him as though she were a "vagabond" (JB). "Wanders" may be translated "veiled," and would suggest a prostitute going from camp to camp. The maiden does not want to give that impression of herself; so she begs her lover to give her the location of his flock.

The Youth's First Response (1:8-11)

Some translators undertake to make the Song of Songs a dramatic dialogue, going so far as to insert in the margins of their translations the designated speakers. Thus the *New International Version* uses the term "Beloved" for the maiden, "Lover" for the youth, and "Friends" for the chorus. *The Jerusalem Bible* uses "The Bride, The Bridegroom, and The Chorus." Such designations are probably suspect upon the basis of scholarship, but they do assist the reader in assigning the various "speeches" of the poems. That one cannot always be certain as to the writer's intention is illustrated by verse 8, which is assigned to "The Chorus" by *The Jerusalem Bible* and to the "Lover" by the *New International Version*. From either one, verse 8 calls to the young maiden that if she will follow the flock's tracks, she will come to the place where the flocks graze and the shepherds pitch their tents.

Verses 9-11 are one of a number of poems describing the maiden's beauty. "Mare" (v. 9b) reflects the fact that she is female, not male. Normally the word would have been *stallion*, for stallions would have drawn the Pharaoh's chariots. Horses were regarded as gallant and beautiful animals, so the young woman is being complimented. Also, it was customary to adorn both horses and women. The ornamented cheeks (v. 10a) refer to the practice of wearing jewelry around the head, with pendants hanging down upon the cheeks.

Dialogue of the Two Lovers (1:12 to 2:2)

Each speaks to the other and is spoken to by the other. She says of him: "My lover is very precious to me. He is like a sachet of myrrh suspended upon a chain and hanging between my breasts. He is as beautiful as a bunch of henna blossoms that grow in Engedi" (v. 12, AT). While the "king" ("lover," shepherd) is lying on his couch, "at his table" (NIV), or in his "room" (JB), the aromatic scent of her perfume reaches him. Myrrh is a perfume made from a shrub which grew in Arabia. It was used at burials, and it was also used in the fertility festivals of Canaanite religion. Henna came from a plant whose powdered leaves were (and still are) used to color the hair. Engedi is a beautiful oasis located near the Dead Sea.

In verse 15 the youth responds by telling the maiden how beautiful she is. "Doves" (v. 15*b*) are frequent representations of femininity and beauty. The dove is also the emblem of purity.

She replies, "And how handsome you are, my lover!" (v. 16, NIV). Reference to their "green" couch suggests that this scene takes place in the woods, the lovers lying on the grass and speaking the age-old love words to one another. Verse 17 may be the lover's response to the beloved's word about the green bed, or it may be a continuation of her thoughts concerning the scene. The beams and rafters mean the branches of the trees that surround them in their love bower.

The allusion to branches of trees might have another meaning, that of the festival of Tabernacles enacted in the fall by the building of a booth or shed composed of tree branches. The family lived in the booth for several days as an annual reminder of their people's homelessness when they were wilderness wanderers. Tabernacles or Booths was also a festival of thanksgiving for the ingathering of the fruit and nuts. The Song of Songs, it is believed by some scholars, was used as part of the liturgy both during Passover and Booths (*Sukkoth*, Hebrew).

In 2:1-2 there is another exchange between the lovers. She says with due feminine modesty, "I am an ordinary flower (lotus, crocus, narcissus—definitely not a 'rose') of the plain, a mere lily of valleys" (AT). This prompts him to reply, "To me you are like a lily among thorns when you are compared with other women" (AT). That was some compliment!

The Maiden Speaks Again (2:3 to 3:5)

Compliments inspire compliments. Her lover called her a lily among thorns. Now she calls him an apple tree among the nondescript trees of the wood. The apple tree as a figure of fruitfulness and beauty was common in the ancient Middle East. The metaphor of the apple tree is carried over into the last two lines of verse 3, as she speaks of sitting in his shade and enjoying the delicious taste of his fruit.

The connection between verses 3 and 4 is made by the thought of the delightful taste of the apples. The maiden describes coming to the house of feasting (v. 4), where love hangs like a banner in a hall. In verse 5 she expresses her hunger for love as though she were famished for food. She is "lovesick" (v. 5c, AT). "Raisins" (v. 5a) may refer to raisin cakes used in the celebration of the fertility cult, for this practice was widely-known in Israel. The tender intimacy of embrace is described in verse 6. The two lovers are pictured as lying on their green couch, the grass, with his left hand under her head and his right arm encircling her.

Verse 7 is addressed to the chorus, "O daughters of Jerusalem," the same words being repeated in 3:5 and 8:4. The meaning of the verse is unclear. Some translators (see James Moffatt) read the verse to admonish not disturbing lovers until "they are satisfied." Others (see NIV and JB) understand the language to say that love should not be aroused prematurely, that it should "awaken when it is ready" (AT). The latter interpretation seems appropriate to this context.

Verses 8-13 are a lyric poem describing a young girl's excitement at the prospect of meeting her lover. The poem has been called "perhaps the most beautiful expression of love in the spring to be found in literature."[1] His strength, youthfulness, and zest are expressed in the figures of his leaping over mountains and bounding over hills (v. 8). Also (v. 9) he is described as a young stag, graceful as a gazelle. He stands outside her house, behind the wall of the courtyard, gazing in her windows, and he calls to her his invitation to come out of the house and run away with him to the hills (v. 10) to see what has happened to make the world beautiful again. Winter is past (v. 11), the winter rains are over, and the drabness of the earth has been transformed into the riot of beauty seen in wild flowers. The earth is pungent with the odor of life and love, the turtledove (v. 12), migrant in Palestine and a harbinger of spring, is once more singing in the land, the fig tree is beginning to produce figs, and the vines are blossoming. The world is alive again after the dull, cold death of winter. It is the time for lovers. "Arise, . . . come away" with me, he calls to her (v. 13).

Verse 14 seems to be a continuation of the lover's invitation to the maiden to come out of her house and risk running away with him to the hills. She is his "dove," a term of endearment, as the dove has often been considered a bird of love. Will she come with him to the hills, to the clefts of the rock and the shadow of the cliff, that he may see her face and enjoy her voice in the secrecy of his hiding place?

Verse 15 is something of a puzzle. "The little foxes" may be understood as those smaller enemies of our best which we are apt to ignore, despite the fact that they can weasel in and "spoil the vineyard" of our lives. What is meant by the young maiden saying, "For our vineyards are in blossom"? Is she referring to her own sanctity and purity? Is she warning her lover that she is tempted in her ripening womanhood by "the little foxes" of other suitors? Any answer is conjectural. The *New International Version* ascribes verse 16 to the man, rather than to the maiden.

In 2:16 to 3:5 we have the maiden's response to her lover's invitation to come away with her to the hills in the springtime. Verse 16 declares their betrothal to one another. "I am his and he is mine" (AT), she says. Verse 17 is her invitation to the lover to come to her before the day breaks while it is still cool, before the shadows flee before the sun. She thinks of him as a beautiful and graceful deer leaping across the hills. The imagery of this verse is such that the reader supplies much of his own interpretation to the language. One thing is certain—it is the language of love.

Chapter 3:1-5 may report the dreams of a girl so much in love that she is lovesick and, waking or sleeping, has her lover on her mind. She dreams that she is searching for him through the streets of the city, but the search is vain. She asks the watchmen if they have seen him, but there is no word of his whereabouts. Suddenly she comes upon him. She is overwhelmed with joy, clinging to him as though never to let him out of her sight again. She takes him home to her mother's house, to the bedroom where she herself was conceived. Verse 5 is a duplicate of 2:7.

A Wedding Song (3:6-11)

A Jewish scholar believes that 3:6-11 contains one of the oldest poems in the Song of Songs, identifying it with the celebration of the marriage of King Solomon to a foreign princess. The bridegroom is seen returning from taking his wife, and his luxurious retinue is described vividly. He is coming from the wilderness (the rough, outlying country), and his long column of guards and attendants make the procession appear to be a column of smoke (v. 6b). They probably were all engulfed in dust. But if you were close to the king's litter (carriage) you would be intoxicated by the fragrance of his perfume. Solomon's opulence was legendary. Two aspects of this royal wedding procession impress the poet. One is the band of armed bodyguards, sixty strong (vv. 7-8), and the other is the richness of his carriage ("palanquin," v. 9). It has silver posts, a gold back, and a purple (color of royalty) seat (v. 10). On the king's head is the crown bestowed upon him by his mother, Bathsheba (v. 11). What a sight! The daughters of Jerusalem are summoned to go out and meet this royal procession as the king returns to his city. This poem may have been originally designed for use in the celebration of a royal marriage, but it is employed here as part of the love talk between the two young lovers.

In verse 8 there is a reference to "alarms by night," which doubtless refers to desert bandits, who might be tempted to attack the king's richly laden caravan bearing a royal princess.

Verse 10 is a graphic description of the luxurious appointments of the king's carriage. One line in the verse, "it was lovingly wrought within," is obscure in the Hebrew text. Does it refer to the loving care of the "daughters of Jerusalem," women who worked in the king's court doing the finishing of the carriage? The Revised Standard Version and *New International Version* give that interpretation of this line. However, *The Jerusalem Bible* and James Moffatt's translations read, "inlaid with ebony." Robert Gordis, a distinguished Jewish scholar, translates the line, "its inner side lined with leather." Which translation is used makes no difference in the sense of the passage, but this is an illustration of the difficulty encountered in translation work.

The "crown" alluded to in verse 11 has an interesting history. It is impossible to say whether the incident being sung about in this poem is literally a reference to Solomon's marriage, or whether the wedding being celebrated is that of two ordinary young people. The reason is that crowns were customarily worn by both groom and bride at their wedding, even if they were peasants. They were king and queen for a day. Their families and friends hailed them as such and gave them gifts as to royalty, toasted them, and rejoiced with them in their marriage.

Praise of the Physical Beauty of the Maiden (4:1-7)

Praise of the bride on her wedding day was a regular feature of Jewish weddings. Two major schools of thought among Jewish scholars spoke of the proper manner in which the bride was to be praised. The school of Shammai, being more conservative, argued that the bride should be saluted only for the qualities which she possessed. The school of Hillel, being more generous and encompassing, took the position that every bride should be addressed as follows: "O bride, beautiful and gracious." In our culture there is a widespread belief that all brides are beautiful on their wedding day.

Do we have in this passage such a song of praise of a bride on her wedding day? We cannot say for sure, inasmuch as the Song of Songs appears to be an anthology of poems about a wide spectrum of man-woman relationships. As one has written, "It contains songs of love's yearning and its consummation, of coquetry and passion, of separation and union, of courtship and marriage."[2] In the present song, the various parts of the maiden's (bride's) physical beauty are hailed and praised.

Verse 1 describes her eyes and her hair. Hebrew poetry is liberally sown with figures of speech, particularly metaphors. The metaphor is especially suited to the style of Hebrew thought and writing, which is highly picturesque, imaginative, yet direct. the noun is much more in evidence than the adjective in Hebrew poetry. Our scientific, factualized orientation of mind makes understanding of Hebrew poetry difficult. We have trouble with metaphors, and are much more comfortable with what we perceive to be factual accounts. Our insistence that things "mean what they say" often leads to our misunderstanding the intentions of the Hebrew poet. He meant what he said, but what he said or wrote can often be understood only in seeing the truth behind the pictures he draws.

Thus, when the maiden's eyes are described as "doves," we have a picture which exudes warmth, love, softness, springtime, beauty. The dove was such a bird. It was identified with expressions of love. And when the maiden's hair is said to be like a flock of goats, a figure we have trouble understanding, the picture is again vivid. The goats would be raven black. As they were herded down a hillside they would give the eye an impression of a woman's long black tresses rippled by the breeze blowing over them.

Verse 2 describes the maiden's beautiful teeth. Why doesn't the poet say to his beloved, "My dear, you have beautiful, even teeth"? He has a much more romantic and picturesque way of saying the same thing which we would reduce to some prosaic remark. To the poet, her teeth are as gleaming white as a flock of freshly-shorn ewes. With the winter's wool sheared, they would be exceptionally white and clean. But more than that, they have just come up from being washed, so their short coats are glistening white. Moreover, they match up like twins! The two rows have not a single gap caused by a missing or crooked tooth. She would be the perfect model for a toothpaste advertisement.

Lips, mouth, and cheeks come next in this catalog of the bride's charms (v. 3). The lips are like a scarlet ribbon (NIV). Was she augmenting their redness, or was it entirely natural? Her mouth is the image of loveliness. Or is it that her "words [are] enchanting" (JB)? The last line of this verse refers to "cheeks" (RSV), or "temples" (KJV, NIV). "Temples" is the preferred translation. "Pomegranates" were common to certain fertility rites, this having to do with the multiplicity of seeds in the pomegranate. Again, we cannot get away entirely from the possibility that these poems were part of a liturgy celebrating fall and spring festivals of the harvest, and that they were subsequently used for more specifically religious purposes.

Reference to the maiden's neck as "like the tower of David" in verse 4 is especially obscure to us. However, a long, graceful neck and a large nose were considered by the ancients to be marks of beauty. The "thousand bucklers" is a reference to the practice of hanging the shields of the army on the walls of the armory when they were not in use. Here the metaphor suggests the necklaces worn by the beautiful woman as part of her dress.

The young woman's breasts are next compared with two fawns, baby deer (v. 5). The imagery is of tenderness, softness, beauty, desirability. Their perfection is expressed in part by their being like identical twins. Again, through the subtlety of imagery the poet writes with grace and yet with a high degree of intimacy. It is the language of love, and it is to be read and understood as such. From time immemorial lovers have said such things to their beloved.

In verse 6 "the mountain of myrrh and the hill of frankincense" are fairly obvious metaphors to describe the body of the beloved. Verse 7 summarizes the entire song of praise for the woman's body. She is "all fair," wholly beautiful. She is "without a blemish" (JB); there is no flaw in her.

"Come with Me, for Your Love Is Supreme" (4:8-15)

Having described his bride's beauty, the bridegroom now calls her to come away with him, and then he once more goes into a rhapsodic description of the wonders of her love. As noted above, the imagery of the language is somewhat provocative to our rather sterile imaginations, especially concerning the vocabulary of love.

Verse 8 contains references to "Lebanon," "Amana," "Senir," and "Hermon." All of these are locations in the north of Palestine, near Syria. It must be noted that Lebanon was closely connected with the Adonis cult, a fertility rite of the Canaanites. It is at least necessary to consider that these songs may have once been used in such rites, later to be taken over by Hebrew liturgists to be part of harvest celebrations.

Amana is the Anti-Lebanon range directly adjacent to the Lebanon range of mountains. Senir and Hermon were mountain peaks.

Verse 9 begins another "confession" of the bridegroom's total enslavement to the love of this woman. She has "stolen" (NIV) his heart away! How many times has that song been sung? With a glance of her eyes, with the flashing of one jewel on her neck, his heart became a captive forever. "My sister, my bride" (v. 9a) is not an unusual way of describing the husband-wife relationship among the ancients, including the Hebrews. Often a man said that his wife was his sister with no intention to deceive—as Abraham had done when he went with Sarah to Egypt.

Verse 10 sings the praise of the maiden's love, better than wine, more intoxicating than the fragrance of any spice. Verse 11 refers to the sweetness of her words. Every word that comes from her lips is sweeter than nectar. "Honey and milk," two highly desirable and delectable foods, are compared with the words on her tongue. Her fragrance is more pungent than the cedar of Lebanon.

Verse 12 contains two figures—"a garden locked" and "a fountain sealed"—which suggest one of two things, or perhaps both. Either the lover is bemoaning the fact that he is being denied access to the beloved, or he is announcing to the world that she belongs to him and is a garden locked and a fountain sealed off against anybody intruding. She belongs to him alone, which is the nature of true fidelity.

"Shoots" in verse 13 is better understood as "tender young plants." The language is highly symbolic, its overall impact being the communication of the uncommon loveliness and fruitfulness of the bride. See note on 4:3 for "pomegranates." The fragrances and spices listed in verse 14 all combine to give the passage the sense of the exotic and mysterious. These are herbs and spices from the East. It is noteworthy that two of them— frankincense and myrrh—are named as among the gifts brought to the Christ child in Bethlehem by the Magi from the East (Matt. 2:11).

Verse 15 completes the lover's description of his beloved. Again in figurative language he describes her abundant gifts. She is a "well of living
water," which means a spring where water comes up out of the ground
and is ever-flowing and fresh, as distinguished from a cistern where the
water is caught and stored and apt to become stagnant. She is a source of
continual refreshment. She is "flowing streams from Lebanon" (v. 15b).
The streams flowing out of the mountains of Lebanon would be cold
and invigorating. They would dance saucily over the rocks as they
rushed toward Galilee, a source of delight and renewal. In such figures
the young lover visualizes and attempts to describe the worth of his beloved.

An Invitation and a Response (4:16 to 5:1)

Verse 16 appears to be the young woman's invitation to her lover. The
language is related to the words by which he described her. If she is a
"garden" to him, let him come to his garden and enjoy its delights, "eat
its choicest fruits" (v. 16b). The vividness and earthiness of these figures
seem self-evident. Without embarrassment, she invites him to enjoy love
with her. Reference to the north and south winds (v. 16a) is to the gentle
breezes that flow back and forth, south and north in Palestine, as opposed to the east wind which blows off the desert and scorches and destroys or the west wind which brings rain from the Mediterranean Sea.

In 5:1 we have the young suitor's reply. He comes to his "garden" and
has his fill of its delights. It is a veritable banquet of good things which
he enjoys to the utmost. Verse 1b is assigned by some translations (NIV)
to the chorus of "Friends." It is in the form of a salute to the two young
lovers to enjoy this banquet together. "Eat . . . and drink . . . your fill,
O lovers" (NIV), they say. This interpretation seems logical, and much
better than trying to explain why the young man would be inviting his
friends to enjoy the delights of his bride.

The Maiden's Fruitless Search for Her Lover (5:2-8)

Here is a highly figurative and imaginative telling of a timeworn
theme of frustrated love. How many times has this story been told in love
songs and popular ballads? The young woman is asleep, but her heart

(mind) is awake. She is restless and full of longing. Suddenly in the darkness there is a knock at her outside door, and she hears her lover's voice. His words are full of passion and desire. "Open to me, my sister, my love," he says. She is also his "dove" and his perfect one. The dew and mist of the night cover him, and he begs her to let him in.

She is overjoyed. Her heart leaps. But she is in bed, she has taken off her robe, and washed her feet (streets were unpaved, floors were earthen). What should she do? She probably did not debate that issue very long, for she was as eager to see him as he was to come to her. But by the time she could get her head clear and get herself properly attired to go to the door he had left in disappointment, thinking that he had been unable to arouse her. She was beside herself. He had been so near, he for whom she longed! He had been there, his hand upon the latch of her door, and now he had gone away. In wild abandon, she ran from her house, unmindful of the night, and began a frantic search for her lover through the streets of her city, calling his name at the top of her lungs. But it is no use. He has gone away, and the lovers, so close to union, are apart. They have missed each other. It is like two lovers agreeing to rendezvous at a given place and one being delayed until the other becomes discouraged and leaves five minutes before the delayed one arrives. How sad, how disappointing!

As she runs through the city the watchmen (local policemen on duty through the night to prevent mischief) see and hear this lone young woman running and crying after a man in the streets. They mistake her for a prostitute, and they treat her roughly as one who deserves no respect. What self-respecting woman would be out running through the streets at night? They beat her and take her coat. In verse 8 she turns to the "chorus," the "daughters of Jerusalem," to implore them to help her in this dire distress. If they should encounter him in the city, will they please give him a message? Tell him that she is beside herself with her love for him. The scene is a tender and moving one. There is nothing cheap about this couple's love. It is an exclusive devotion, each to the other. That is the kind of married love the Bible honors and commands. It is the love of a Ruth and Boaz, of an Isaac and Rebekah, of a Jacob and Rachel. "Therefore a man leaves his father and his mother and cleaves to his wife, and they become one flesh" (Gen. 2:24). There is nothing tawdry, and nothing otherworldly, about those words. They are plain and explicit. They say what they mean and mean what they say.

A Word from the Chorus (5:9)

If this is indeed a kind of dramatic dialogue, as some interpreters hold, the role of the chorus is to reflect upon what is happening concerning the major characters, in this case the lover and the beloved. Here they ask her what is so special about her lover that they should be concerned to help her find him. This gives her the occasion to describe his good qualities, as he has previously described hers.

Praise of the Young Man's Physical Beauty (5:10-16)

What is special about him? Everything! He is one in ten thousand! That is special enough. His head, his hair, his eyes, his cheeks, his lips, his arms, his body (trunk), his legs, his entire body, his speech—all are most desirable. Note how she reports his physical attributes from head to foot. She passes down his body in her mind's eye and sees only perfection at every point. All is seen in superlatives. His head is gold; his hair is as wavy and black as a raven's coat; his eyes are like doves (see his description of her eyes); his cheeks are as pretty as a bed of spices growing; his lips are as lovely as lilies blooming and giving off fragrance; his arms are smooth and precious as gold, his body as ivory; his legs are strong and beautiful like alabaster columns; his feet are like gold. He is as tall as a cedar of Lebanon, and his speech is like liquid music. "O daughters of Jerusalem, this is what my lover and friend is like. Do you wonder that I adore him?" (v. 16b, AT).

Another Word from the Chorus and the Maiden's Response (6:1-3)

The chorus asks her in verse 1, "Where has he gone?" They are willing to help her find him if she has some idea where he is.

Her response is in verses 2-3. He has gone to his gardens to pasture his flock. The symbolism of this statement is obscure. Does she mean that he has sought other sources of refreshment and comfort? Not likely, as verse 3 makes explicit. In this verse she reaffirms her devotion to him and his to her. "I am his and he is mine," she says, lest there be any suspicion that the two have parted ways.

The Lover Praises the Unique Beauty of His Bride (6:4-10)

Here is another love song (see 4:1-15) devoted to praise of the beauty of the beloved. "Tirzah" (v. 1) was once the capital of the Northern Kingdom of Israel, as Jerusalem was the capital of Judah. Does this suggest that the song comes from the north?

The dazzling beauty and compelling eyes of this woman make her admirer uncomfortable. She is too much for him! He begs her (as an expression of his ardor) to avert her gaze (v. 5). It is so powerful and penetrating that he becomes flustered like a schoolboy on his first date. He can't think or talk straight if she is looking at him. Verses 5b-7 repeat the language of 4:1b-3, except for 4:3a which is not found in the standard Hebrew text but was included in the Greek translation called the Septuagint (second century BC).

Verse 8 is obscure. It must have some reference to King Solomon's court and his many wives and concubines. When taken with verse 9 it may be saying that although Solomon could take his pick among many wives and concubines, the one he really is overcome by is this simple, swarthy maiden whom he finds irresistible. Not only did her mother think that she was the prettiest thing she ever saw (don't all mothers think that about their daughters?), but the other women admired her beauty, too (v. 9). However, the "king" was the one who chose her above others, and praised her beauty, as in verse 10.

The Beloved Visits the Garden (6:11-12)

These two verses are unusually difficult. To begin with, translators do not agree as to the identity of the speaker. Is it the maiden (*Interpreter's Bible*), or the man (NIV, TEV, JB)? This expositor believes that the lines belong to the maiden. She reports that she visited the orchard (garden) to see whether the trees had budded and the flowers had burst forth. In short, she went to see whether spring had come. The connection between the rites of spring and the "coming of love" is legendary. Verse 12 has been cited by translators as hopelessly confused. None of the translations seem to do the language justice. Some (NIV, TEV) attribute the words to the young man (as does also *The Jerusalem Bible*). But even they do not agree as to what the words say. The Revised Standard Version has the words coming from the maiden who says something to the effect that her "fancy" (imagination?) took her unaware and set her in a chariot beside her prince. James Moffatt's translation simply omits the verse, noting and numbering the place, but making no effort at translating it.

The Chorus Speaks and the Maiden Replies (6:13)

Verse 13 contains a call to the young woman, issued by the chorus. She is dancing, evidently her wedding dance, as there is to this day among certain Syrian groups the practice of the bride performing a sword dance on her wedding day. This may be a Hebrew version of that custom. The chorus says to her, "Turn around, turn around, that we may gaze upon your beauty!" (AT).

The second part of this verse is considered by many interpreters to be the maiden's reply. Modestly she asks why they want to look at her. What virtue and grace can they possibly see in one so simple and unsophisticated as she? "Shulammite" has sometimes been identified with Abishag the Shunammite, David's last female companion (see 1 Kings 1:3-4), but this is almost certainly inaccurate. Others have understood the word to be a feminine form of Solomon, but that seems improbable. The dance she performs may have been a special dance performed as though before an army, but more likely done at a wedding feast.

The Maiden's Dance Arouses Her Lover (7:1-9)

The language of this poem is graphic and sensual. Nothing less can be made of it while being faithful to the text. Whereas the lover had earlier described his beloved's beauty by beginning with her eyes and face and working down her body, here he begins with her feet and works up.

Her feet are beautiful in their sandals. Not everyone has pretty feet. The curve of her thighs is so perfect that it looks as though a master sculptor had made them. Her "navel" (literally, her genital area) is like a "rounded bowl," always full of mixed wine. Her belly is like a sheaf of wheat (golden, ripe, fruitful), surrounded by beauty as of lilies. Verse 3 is repeated from 4:5, leaving off the last line of 4:5. Her neck (v. 4a) is like an ivory tower, white and smooth and stately. Her eyes are as deep and mysterious as the water pools of Heshbon (a city east of Jordan). The reference to "Bath-rabbim" is obscure. Her nose (v. 4c) is as straight and impressive-looking as a tower of Lebanon overlooking and guarding the city of Damascus.

Her head (v. 6) is a crown upon this beautiful body, as Mount Carmel is a crown rising above the valley of Jezreel. Her flowing tresses are so jet black that they seem to give off a purple hue. They are so intriguing that the sight of them captivates a king. Verse 6 is a refrain repeating her loveliness, as though he is about to launch into a "second stanza" of his song, which is precisely what he does.

Verse 7 compares her stateliness to that of a palm tree, her breasts to its clusters of dates. Verse 8 is explicit. He says to himself, "I will climb the palm tree and pick its fruit" (TEV). Then he changes the metaphor from clusters of palms to bunches of grapes on the vine (v. 8b). Moreover, her breath is as sweet as the fragrance of apples, her kisses as delectable as the finest wine that smoothly pleases the palate and glides over lips and teeth (v. 9). Such was his response to watching the beauty of her dancing form. The speech is earthy, but in no sense ugly or cheap.

The Maiden Invites the Lover into the Fields and Desires to Marry Him (7:10 to 8:4)

The maiden's response is to declare her loyal commitment to her beloved. He desires her, and she is glad to be wanted (v. 10). On the strength of that mutual commitment and dedication, each to the other, she invites him to come with her to the countryside to see and enjoy the glorious beauty and wonder of spring. Picture the two young lovers strolling hand in hand or arm in arm down the lane to the glorious burst of spring. It is the season for young love. Are the vines budding? Are their blossoms on them? Have the pomegranates put forth their blooms? Pomegranates, full of seeds, symbolized fertility. There amidst the bursting new life of God's natural order she plans to "give you my love." It is an offer based upon the pure love which she has for the man who has chosen her and whom she has chosen, rather than a cheap display of carnality.

The mandrakes (v. 13) were highly regarded for their power to stimulate sexual desire (see Gen. 30:14-16). The fruit growing around the door may have the significance of the maiden's complete dedication of herself to her husband-to-be.

Has this maiden experienced criticism from her neighbors because of her bold public expression of affection for her hero? Perhaps. If only her lover were a half-brother—one nursed by her mother—the gossips would have nothing to talk about. She could kiss him without being criticized (8:1). Further, she could take him to her mother's house and share a cup of wine with him without endangering her good name (v. 2). Verses 3-4 are repeated from 2:6-7 except for the omission of one line: "By the gazelles or hinds of the field." Here, as there, the language of embrace is explicit in the first verse, and in the second the meaning appears to be that love should not be aroused too soon, that it should be left "asleep" until it is possible and appropriate to release the power that it contains. "For everything there is a season" (Eccl. 3:1).

The Chorus Sees the Two Lovers Returning (8:5a)

This brief interjection by the singers who repeat and facilitate the movements of the lover and beloved is designed to explain that the two lovers are now together. The chorus simply announces them, much as a herald might announce the approach of the royal family.

The Maiden Pleads with Her Lover to Be Faithful (8:5b-7)

As she comes back from the wilderness, she is addressing her lover. She reminds him that she woke him from sleep under the apple tree, and again alludes to the place as the site of his birth. The reason for associating his birth with their love (see 8:2) is unclear. We do know that fruit trees, especially apple, were thought of as having special significance to fertility. As early in the Old Testament as Genesis 3 and the Garden of Eden, the "forbidden fruit" has been cited as having certain sexual implications.

Verse 6 alludes to an ancient custom of carrying a seal suspended by a chain around the neck, or from the arm. The seal served the purpose of a signature to any document which needed signing. Inasmuch as few people could write, the seal was the official documentation. The figure is used here to press upon the young man his beloved's desire that he be faithful to her. "Let me be the seal you wear around your neck or on your arm" (AT). One translator puts it as follows: "Close your heart to every love but mine; hold no one in your arms but me" (TEV). That rendering is not literal, but it is faithful to the text.

Verses 6-7 amplify the plea for faithfulness to the love relationship. "Love is strong as death," she says. Surely no statement in all the literature of love would find greater consensus of agreement. "Till death us do part" has been repeated in the marriage vows of countless couples for centuries. Sad is the day when people begin to hedge on that promise and to scale it down to mean something other than total and lifelong commitment. "Jealousy" (RSV) is not a good translation of the Hebrew word. A better is "passion." Passion is not so much "cruel" (RSV) as "adamant, relentless" as death. As no one can escape death, so no one can elude the devotion of a genuine passion. Passion is like a raging fire that cannot be extinguished (v. 6c). Verse 7 continues the thought with the hyperbole of love's quenchless tenacity. Not even floods can drown the raging fire of love. What is so mysterious about this force of love is that it exists without calculation. One cannot buy love, even if all the wealth of one's house were offered. Genuine love is not for sale. It is a bestowal.

The Chorus Describes the Chastity of the Beloved (8:8-9)

These two verses are problematic. Some translators assign them to the maiden's brothers (TEV), but that seems unnecessary and unlikely, inasmuch as the chorus is already a part of this dramatic dialogue and could well be given the lines. The lines speak of the chastity of the beloved, the maiden, and not of a younger sister at home. "She has no breasts" refers, of course, to her earlier stage when she was a little girl. The question is, "How shall we protect our little sister when young men come a-courting?" The wall and the gate are symbolic allusions to her sexual parts. This maiden is to be protected, her virtue and chastity preserved. A silver battlement (breastworks?) will be erected to protect her wall, and boards of cedar to defend her gate. In short, she will have the active involvement of her family in preserving her chastity until the time of marriage. These verses reflect backward upon the way she was brought up. Now she is ready for marriage to her lover, and she offers him her chastity.

The Maiden Offers Herself as a Chaste Woman (8:10-12)

The maiden now declares that she does in fact bring to her lover a chaste body. Again "wall" and "towers" are sexual allusions to her purity. She has kept herself morally straight, therefore she is a source of peace and contentment to her husband (v. 10).

Verses 11-12 refer back to the statement about the unpurchasable nature of love (v. 7b). Here reference is made to Solomon's great wealth and his renting or leasing his vineyards. The maiden says, "My vineyard is not for sale. It is my very own, and I shall keep it for myself until I am ready to give it to the one I love" (v. 12, AT). Hers is an admirable and beautiful statement of her womanly virtue.

The Lover Calls and the Maiden Replies (8:13-14)

The closing lines are love calls, each calling to the other. He says, "My friends have heard so much about you from me. Come, let them see you and hear your voice" (v. 13, AT). He is proud of his betrothed and, like any proud bridegroom, he wants to "show her off."

Her response is to call to him and tell him to hurry to her, that she is eager for his arms. "Gazelle" and "young stag" are vivid figures of grace and swiftness. She is impatient for the union of their loves and lives, and the love languages closes with her invitation to him not to delay coming to her side.

Notes

1. Robert Gordis, *The Song of Songs and Lamentations* (New York: KTAV Publishing House, Inc., 1974), p. 52.

2. Ibid., p. 18.

Bibliography

Allen, Clifton J., Ed. *The Broadman Bible Commentary*, V. Nashville: Broadman Press, 1971.

Buttrick, George Arthur, Ed. *The Interpreter's Bible*, IV and V. New York: Abingdon Press, 1956.

Crenshaw, James L. *Old Testament Wisdom: An Introduction.* Atlanta: John Knox Press, 1981.

Ginsburg, Christian D. *The Song of Songs and Coheleth.* New York: KTAV Publishing House, Inc., 1970.

Gordis, Robert. *The Song of Songs and Lamentations.* New York: KTAV Publishing House, Inc., 1974.

Johnson, L. D. *Israel's Wisdom: Learn and Live.* Nashville: Broadman Press, 1975.

Noth, Martin and D. Winton Thomas, Eds. *Wisdom in Israel and in the Ancient Near East.* Leiden: E. J. Brill, 1955.

Rad, Gerhard von. *Wisdom in Israel.* London: SCM Press, Ltd., 1972.

Scott, R. B. Y. *Proverbs, Ecclesiastes, The Anchor Bible.* Garden City, New York: Doubleday & Co., 1965.

_____. *The Way of Wisdom in the Old Testament.* New York: Macmillan Co., 1971.

Wilkin, Robert L., Ed. *Aspects of Wisdom in Judaism and Early Christianity.* London: University of Notre Dame Press, 1975.